THE COMPLETE
LATIN
FOR ALL
OCCASIONS

Also by Henry Beard
Alii libri qui ab Henrico Barbato scripti sunt

Miss Piggy's Guide to Life
Sailing: A Sailor's Dictionary
Fishing: An Angler's Dictionary
Golfing: A Duffer's Dictionary
Skiing: A Skier's Dictionary

HENRY BEARD

THE COMPLETE LATIN FOR ALL OCCASIONS

Lingua Latina occasionibus omnibus in toto

Everything you'll ever need to say in perfect Latin

LONDON   NEW YORK   SYDNEY   TORONTO

This omnibus edition published 1995
by BCA
by arrangement with HarperCollins Publishers

First Reprint 1995

CN 1630

Printed and bound in Great Britain by
Mackays of Chatham PLC, Chatham, Kent

CONTENTS

LATIN FOR ALL OCCASIONS

Lingua Latina Occasionibus Omnibus

Was I speaking Latin again?
Denuone Latine loquebar?

Silly me. Sometimes it just sort of slips out.
Me ineptum. Interdum modo elabitur.

PREFACE
Praefatio

You know the feeling all too well. There you are, chatting with business associates at an upscale watering hole, or participating in a little good-natured give-and-take during a golf or tennis match, or relaxing with friends on the beach, or maybe just reviewing the day with your family at the supper table. You spot a chance to liven up the discussion with a particularly pithy observation in Latin, and then, all of a sudden, you're assailed by paralyzing doubts.

Is the verb you were going to use in the second or third conjugation? Is it irregular? Deponent? Reflexive? Defective? Does it take *ut* and a subjunctive or an infinitive with an accusative? Or, worse still, does it take the dative? Would a gerundive construction be more appropriate, or laughably awkward? How about a passive periphrastic or—but no, it's too late. The moment has passed, the conversation has moved on.

Now be honest—how many times has that happened to you? If you answer is *saepius* (too often)—and we bet it is!—then *Lingua Latin Occasionibus Omnibus* (Latin for All Occasions) is the book for you.

Here, in one handy, easy-to-use volume, are hundreds of everyday English expressions rendered into grammatically accurate, idiomatically correct classical Latin, just as you would have translated them yourself if you had the time. And all of these practical phrases are conveniently organized into familiar conversational categories so that you can be confident that in any social situation some suitable Latin *bona dicta* (bon mots) will be right at your fingertips, just the way they would be if you could only get in a little practice.

The next time you feel like using the immortal language of Caesar, Cicero, Virgil, and Horace to turn an ordinary remark into a timeless utterance, don't let *feles, felis, feli, felem, fele* (the cat) get your tongue. With a copy of *Lingua Latina Occasionibus Omnibus* (Latin for All Occasions) in your toga, you'll never again be intimidated by those seven hundred verb endings, ninety noun cases, and twenty kinds of ablative. And you'll quickly discover that whether you want to impress the boss, entertain your friends, keep the kids in line, or charm that special someone, speaking Latin is as easy as taking Gaul from the Gauls!

Bona fortuna! (Good luck!)

ACKNOWLEDGMENTS
Gratiae

I would like to thank Mark Sugars and Winifred Lewellen, who reviewed my Latin for accuracy and appropriateness. Their many corrections and suggestions greatly improved this book, and no doubt spared me untold grief from outraged Latin teachers. To these two distinguished classical scholars belongs much of the credit for any felicity of style or elegance of diction; the *culpa* for any mistakes is entirely *mea*.

CONTENTS
Quad in libro continetur

INTRODUCTION:
A BRIEF GUIDE TO
LATIN PRONUNCIATION

*Prooemium: Locutio linguae Latinae
paucis verbis explanatur*

If it's been a few years since you last conversed in Latin regularly, your pronunciation may have gotten a bit rusty, so we've included here a short summary of the basics of the spoken language just to help you brush up a little.

A word of caution: This is a simplified system of pronunciation for colloquial Latin based in part on modern Italian, the direct vernacular descendant of the everyday speech of ancient Rome. If you're planning to give a formal oration or a reading from one of the great works of classical literature, you're obviously going to want to consult the standard scholarly reference books for the proper literary pronunciation.

I VOWELS AND A FEW DIPTHONGS

Sure, I speak a little Latin.

- *Sane, paululum linguae Latinae dico.*
  SAH-nay, pow-LOO-luhm LEEN-gwye Lah-TEE-nye DEE-koh.

A   is pronounced "ah" as in "father."

E   is pronounced "ay" as in "they," but the very common words
    et (and), est (is), and sed (but) should be pronounced like "bet,"
    "best," and "said," and the very common word ending em
    should be pronounced like "stem."

I   is pronounced "ee" as in "Vaseline," but the very common words <u>i</u>d (it) and <u>i</u>n (in, on) should be pronounced like "d<u>i</u>d" and "d<u>i</u>n."

O   is pronounced "oh" as in "g<u>o</u>."

U   is pronounced "oo" as in "cr<u>u</u>de," but the very common word endings <u>us</u> and <u>um</u> shuld be pronounced like "p<u>us</u>s" and "r<u>oo</u>m" (with the "oo" sound of "c<u>oo</u>kb<u>oo</u>k"), and the very common word <u>ut</u> (how, so that) should be pronounced like "p<u>u</u>t."

AE   is a dipthong (a pair of vowels joined together to form a single sound) pronounced "eye."

AU   is a dipthong pronounced "ow," as in "lu<u>au</u>."

OE   is a dipthong pronounced "oy."

II Consonants

I picked it up here and there. Really, Latin isn't all that hard.
- *Id legi modo hic modo illic. Vero, Latine loqui non est difficilissimum.*

   IDD LAY-gee MOH-doh HEEK MOH-doh EEL-leek. WAY-roh, Lah-TEE-nay LOH-kwee NOHN EHSST dee-fee-kee-LEESE-see-muhm.

B, D, F, H, K, L, M, N, P, and Z all sound the same as they do in English.

C   always has a "K" sound as in "<u>c</u>ar."

Ch   always has a "K" sound as in "<u>ch</u>orus."

G   always has a hard "G" sound as in "<u>g</u>et."

Gu   is pronounced "Gw" when it comes after an "n," as it is in English.

I   is a consonant pronounced like "Y" when it is the first letter in a word and it is followed by a vowel. The common Latin word <u>iam</u> (now) is pronounced "YAHM."

Qu   is pronounced "Kw," as it is in English.

R   can be rolled in a sort of Scottish burr.

S   always has a hissing sound as in "moo<u>s</u>e" or "<u>s</u>oda," and some very common word endings sound like this: <u>as</u> = "demi-ta<u>sse</u>"; <u>es</u> = "<u>ace</u>"; <u>is</u> = "g<u>eese</u>"; <u>os</u> = "verb<u>ose</u>"; and <u>us</u> = "w<u>uss</u>."

T   always has a hard "T" sound as in "tar." In Latin, the word "ratio" is pronounced "RAH-tee-oh."

V   is always pronounced as if it were a "W." What Caesar (KYE-sahr) said after he defeated somebody or other (veni, vidi, vici) sounded as if he had just conquered Hawaii: WAY-nee, WEE-dee, WEE-kee.*

X   is always pronounced "Ks."

J, W, and Y don't exist in Latin.

III Syllables

It looks like a tricky language, but you'll get the hang of it pretty quickly.

- *Lingua speciem involutam praebet, sed sat cito eam comprehendes.*
  LEEN-gwah SPAY-kee-ehm inn-woh-LOO-tahm PRYE-bayt, SEDD SAHT KEE-toh AY-ahm kohm-pray-HAYN-dace.

Latin words are divided into syllables in the same way that English words are, but in Latin every vowel or dipthong is a syllable, and every syllable is pronounced separately. If there are two vowels together, and they are not AE, AU, or OE, both vowels are pronounced individually. So, for example, <u>praebat</u> = "PRYE-baht" (<u>ae</u> is a dipthong); <u>speciem</u> = "SPAY-kee-ehm"; and <u>eam</u> = "AY-ahm."

* If you took Latin in a parochial school, you were probably taught to pronounce the letter "V" like the English "V," the dipthong "ae" like "sun<u>dae</u>", and Caesar like "CHAY-sahr." If you do this, you are going to take <u>s</u>ome flak from Latin purists, classics snobs, and other assorted lingo bores, but on the other hand, you're going to get a much better table in the Vatican restaurant.

IV STRESS

And remember, there aren't any Romans around to correct
your pronunciation.

- *Atque memento, nulli adsunt Romanorum qui locutionem tuam
corrigant.*

   AHT-kway may-MAYN-toh, NOO-lee AHD-soont Roh-mah-
   NOH-ruhm KWEE loh-koo-tee-OH-nehm TOO-ahm KOH-
   ree-gahnt.

If a word has two syllables, put the stress on the first one. If it has
more than two, put the stress on the second-to-last syllable unless
both the second-to-last syllable and the last syllable are vowels.
When that happens, shift the stress back one syllable earlier.

So, for example, locutionem = "loh-koo-tee-OH-nehm," but locutio = "loh-KOO-tee-oh."

If the second-to-last syllable has an "i" in it and doesn't end in
a consonant, the stress is usually moved back one syllable. So, for
example, corrigant = "KOHR-ree-gahnt" and dificilissimum =
"dee-fee-kee-LEESE-ee-muhm." For the same reason, the very common word aliqui (any) is pronounced "AH-lee-kwee."

I.

CONVERSATIONAL LATIN

Lingua Latina Conlocutioni

Cocktail Party Chitchat

Hot enough for you?
- *Satine caloris tibi est?*

Run into much traffic on the way over?
- *Turbane magna vehiculorum obviam erat tibi venienti huc?*

What do you think I paid for this watch?
- *Quanto putas mihi stare hoc horologium manuale?*

You know what I think? I think . . .
- *Visne scire quod credam? Credo . . .*

> . . . that all wrestling is fixed.
> . . . *luctationes omnes praestitutas esse.*

> . . . that flying saucers are real.
> . . . *orbes volantes exstare.*

> . . . that Elvis is still alive.
> . . . *Elvem ipsum etiam vivere.*

> . . . that the weather has been altered by rocket launches.
> . . . *missiones turrium flammearum statum caeli mutavisse.*

> . . . that no one's barbecue sauce is better than mine.
> . . . *condimentum pro carne in veribus cocta nullius praestare ei mei.*

CONVERSATION FILLERS

Is that so?
- *Ain tu?*

Really?
- *Vero?*

You don't say!
- *Dic! Itane est?*

You can say that again!
- *Illud iterum dicere potes!*

You know what they say . . .
- *Scis quod dicunt . . .*

     . . . here today, gone tomorrow.
     . . . hodie adsit, cras absit.

     . . . seen one, seen them all.
     . . . uno viso, omnia visa sunt.

     . . . what goes around, comes around.
     . . . id quod circumiret, circumveniat.

     . . . que sera, sera.
     . . . quod fiat, fiat.

CONVERSATION ENDERS

God, look at the time! My wife will kill me!
- *Di! Ecce hora! Uxor mea me necabit!*

Excuse me. I've got to see a man about a dog.
- *Mihi ignosce. Cum homine de cane debeo congredi.*

Darn! There goes my beeper!
- *Heu! Tintinnuntius meus sonat!*

I'm outta here.
- *Abeo.*

Have a nice day.
- *Die dulci fruere.*

Pithy Latin Expressions to Use in English

Ipso facto
- By that very fact

Nullo modo
- No way

Labra lege.
- Read my lips.

Pactum factum
- A done deal

Fors fortis
- Fat chance

Casu consulto
- Accidentally on purpose

Raptus regaliter
- Royally screwed

Totus anctus
- In a world of hurt

Utinam
- Hopefully

II.
NFORMATIONAL LATIN
Lingua Latina Nuntiis

LATIN SIGNS FOR OUR TIMES

CAVE CANEM
- BEWARE OF DOG

NOLI PERTURBARE
- DO NOT DISTURB

NOLI INTRARE
- KEEP OUT

OPORTET MINISTROS MANUS LAVARE ANTEQUAM LATRINAM RELINQUENT
- EMPLOYEES MUST WASH HANDS BEFORE LEAVING RESTROOM

BARBARI! IN HOC CURRU NULLA ARCA SONORUM ADSIT!
- NO RADIO!

TIBI GRATIAS AGIMUS QUOD NIHIL FUMAS
- THANK YOU FOR NOT SMOKING

SI HOC SIGNUM LEGERE POTES, OPERIS BONI IN REBUS LATINIS ALACRIBUS ET FRUCTUOSIS POTIRI POTES!
- IF YOU CAN READ THIS SIGN, YOU CAN GET A GOOD JOB IN THE FAST-PACED, HIGH-PAYING WORLD OF LATIN!

Latin Bumper Stickers for Your Chariot

FRENA PRO FERIS TENEO
- I BRAKE FOR ANIMALS

BALAENAE NOBIS CONSERVANDAE SUNT
- SAVE THE WHALES

SONA SI LATINE LOQUERIS
- HONK IF YOU SPEAK LATIN

CUM CATAPULTAE PROSCRIPTAE ERUNT TUM SOLI PROSCRIPTI CATAPULTAS HABEBUNT
- WHEN CATAPULTS ARE OUTLAWED, ONLY OUTLAWS WILL HAVE CATAPULTS

SI HOC ADFIXUM IN OBICE LEGERE POTES, ET LIBERALITER EDUCATUS ET NIMIS PROPINQUUS ADES
- IF YOU CAN READ THIS BUMPER STICKER, YOU ARE BOTH VERY WELL EDUCATED AND MUCH TOO CLOSE

VANITAS PLATES

INCITATUS
- SPEED DEMON

VAGANS
- CRUISING

LITORALIS
- BEACH BUM

MANNUS
- MUSTANG

FRACTUM
- JALOPY

NITIDUS
- SNAZZY

URSUS
- BEAR

AMO VI-UM
- I LOVE SEX

TURBO
- TURBO

LATIN AS A COMPUTER LANGUAGE

Why won't you print out?
- *Cur ullum imprimere non vis?*

Don't you dare erase my hard disk!
- *Ne auderis delere orbem rigidum meum!*

I did not commit a fatal error!
- *Non erravi perniciose!*

Garbage in, garbage out.
- *Purgamentum init, exit purgamentum.*

AN ALL-PURPOSE PERSONAL AD

Attractive and intelligent man/woman wishes to meet a Latin speaker of the opposite sex. Please—no pig Latin!

Vir/mulier iucundus/iucunda intellegensque vult obviam convenire alicui sexus adversi qui lingua Latina utitur. Amabo—nihil loquelae Latinae suillae!

AN ALL-PURPOSE LETTER

Dear Sir:
I have received your letter and I will give the matter to which you referred my promptest and fullest attention.

                Best wishes,

Dominus meus:
Epistulam tuam accepi et rei cuius mentionem ibi fecisti animadversionem meam promptissimam plenissimamque dabo.

                Semper vale et salve,

AN ALL-PURPOSE POSTCARD MESSAGE

Having a wonderful time. I wish you were here. Or should it be, I should wish you had been here? Or maybe, I should have been wishing that you had been here? Or, I did wish you to have been here?

                Best,

Tempus dulcissime oblecto. Volo ut mecum adsis. Aut debetne dicere, Velim ut mecum aderis? Aut fortasse, Vellem ut mecum adfueris? Aut, Volui te mecum adfuisse?

                Optationes optimas ad te,

AN ALL-PURPOSE ANSWERING-MACHINE MESSAGE

Hello. No one can come to the phone right now to take your call, but you can leave a message if you want by speaking as soon as you hear the beep. Remember to wait for the beep. Bye.

Salve. Nemo nunc ipsum advenire ad longelocutum ad vocem tuam accipiendam potest, sed possis si velis nuntiam tradere dicendo simul ac sonitum audiveris. Memento sonitu praestolare. Ave.

AN ALL-PURPOSE TELEPHONE PRANK

Hello, is this the supermarket? Do you have Janitor in a Drum and Mr. Clean in a bottle? You do? Well, let them out! Ha ha ha!

Dic, estne magnimercatus? Estne vobis Ianitor in Cupa et Magister Purus in ampulla? Sicine? Bene, eos emitte! Hae hae hae!

AN ALL-PURPOSE STICK-UP NOTE

I have a catapult. Give me all the money, or I will fling an enormous rock at your head.

Catapultam habeo. Nisi pecuniam omnem mihi dabis, ad caput tuum saxum immane mittam.

NEGOTIATING IN LATIN

I'd like to cut a deal.
- *Volo pactum facere.*

Now this isn't carved in stone.
- *Nunc hoc in marmore non est incisum.*

This is just a ballpark figure.
- *Hic est numerus, plus aut minus.*

I'm thinking out loud.
- *Clara voce cogito.*

This is all blue sky.
- *Totum de caelo caeruleo venit.*

I think we're on the same wavelength.
- *Credo nos in fluctu eodem esse.*

Sweetening the Deal

Can you put more money on the table?
- *Potesne plus pecuniae in mensa ponere?*

Let's look at the bottom line.
- *Summam scrutemur.*

Is that your best offer?
- *Num ista condicio optima est?*

Can't you sharpen up your pencil a little on this?
- *Nonne potes stilum tuum in hac re paulum acuere?*

If you can't go any higher, the deal is off.
- *Si plus offerre non potes, pactum ruptum est.*

Playing Hardball

We're back to square one.
- *In carceribus denuo adsumus.*

I'm wasting my time.
- *Tempus meum tero.*

That's the deal. Take it or leave it.
- *Ecce pactum. Id cape aut id relinque.*

You're not the only game in town.
- *In oppido lusor solus non es.*

Well, you win some, you lose some.
- *Modo vincis, modo vinceris.*

HIDDEN INSULTS

LATIN	WHAT YOU SAY IT MEANS	WHAT IT REALLY MEANS
Podex perfectus es.	You did a terrific job.	You are a total asshole.
De stella Martis vere venisti.	That's a truly remarkable insight.	You are definitely from Mars.
Stercorem pro cerebro habes.	That's certainly food for thought.	You have shit for brains.
Caput tuum in ano est.	You hit the nail right on the head.	You have your head up your ass.
Futue te ipsum et caballum tuum.	I've really got to take my hat off to you.	Screw you and the horse you rode in on.

USEFUL BUSINESS EXPRESSIONS

Take the bull by the horns.
- *Taurum per cornua prehende.*

It comes with the territory.
- *Cum tractu traducto.*

Give me a little feedback.
- *Dic mihi paulum quod sentis.*

If it ain't broke, don't fix it.
- *Si fractum non sit, noli id reficere.*

Get your ducks in a row.
- *Anates tuas in acie instrue.*

The ball is in your court.
- *Pila in area tua est.*

I'm up the creek without a paddle.
- *In rivo fimi sine remo sum.*

It ain't over until it's over.
- *Id imperfectum manet dum confectum erit.*

Making a Cold Call

I'd like to bounce something off you.
- *Aliquo te volo petere.*

You seem like someone who knows a good thing when he
    sees it.
- *Tute videris esse qui noscat rem bonam cum videat.*

It's a once-in-a-lifetime opportunity.
- *Occasio rarissima est.*

I'm sorry we couldn't do business.
- *Stercorem pro cerebro habes.* *

* See Hidden Insults, p. 19

THE UNA-MINUTIA MANAGER

Take a letter.
- *Scribe.*

Xerox(R) this.
- *Huius Xerographiam(P) fac.*

Hold my calls.
- *Fac ut nemo me vocet.*

I don't get headaches. I give them.
- *Dolores capitis non fero. Eos do.*

The buck stops here.
- *Denarius hic sistit.*

There's no free lunch.
- *Nulla mensa sine impensa.*

You're fired.
- *Ego te demitto.*

Mogul Jargon

Let's take a meeting.
- *Congressum faciamus.*

Have your people talk to my people.
- *Tuos iube meis dicere.*

What's the net-net on this?
- *Quid in re reditum residuum reliquumque restat?*

It's the standard deal.
- *Conventum consuetum est.*

Baby, sweetheart, would I lie to you?
- *Amicule, deliciae, num is sum qui mentiar tibi?*

Let's cut to the chase.
- *Ad venatum vadamus.*

Don't pass on this!
- *Noli hoc praeterire!*

Give me a green light!
- *Da mihi lumen viride!*

You're beautiful!
- *Pulcher es!*

Let's have lunch, really!
- *Prandeamus, vere!*

IV.
RECREATIONAL LATIN
Lingua Latina Oblectamentis

At the Football Stadium

These are great seats, aren't they?
- *Sedilia haec, nonne praestant?*

First and ten, do it again! Touchdown!
- *Primum et decem est, rursum agendum est! Detractum!*

God, these halftime shows are boring.
- *Hercle, ludicra haec inter dimidia muneris intercedentia insulsa sunt.*

At the Ball Park

I hate Astroturf.
- *Gramen artificiosum odi.*

The designated-hitter rule has got to go.
- *Lex clavatoris designati rescindenda est.*

The best baseball stadium is still Fenway Park.
- *Stadium sedipilae optimum Saeptum Paludosum etiamnunc est.*

CHEERING FOR YOUR TEAM

Let's go . . .
• *Eamus, O . . .*

AMERICAN LEAGUE/EAST

Orioles	*Icteri Galbuli*
Yankees	*Ianqui*
Blue Jays	*Cyanocittae Cristatae*
Brewers	*Fermentatores*
Red Sox	*Tibialia Rubentia*
Indians	*Indi*
Tigers	*Tigres*

AMERICAN LEAGUE/WEST

A's	*Athletici*
Angels	*Angeli*
Royals	*Regii*
Rangers	*Equites*
Twins	*Gemini*
Mariners	*Nautae*
White Sox	*Tibialia Alba*

NATIONAL LEAGUE/EAST

Expos	*Expositiones*
Mets	*Metropolitae*
Cubs	*Catuli*
Cardinals	*Cardinales*
Pirates	*Piratae*
Phillies	*Philadelphii*

Giants	*Gigantes*
Astros	*Astrotholi Incolae*
Reds	*Rubri*
Dodgers	*Elusores*
Padres	*Patri*
Braves	*Fortes*

AT A HOCKEY GAME

Hockey fans are real animals.
- *Fautores ludi glacialis Borei feri meri sunt.*

Here comes the Zamboni.
- *Huc accedit Zambonis.*

AT THE POKER TABLE

Read 'em and weep.
- *Lege atque lacrima.*

This isn't a hand, it's a foot.
- *Hoc non manus sed pes est.*

On the Golf Course

I'm going to take a Mulligan.
- *Alterum ictum faciam.*

We're playing winter rules, aren't we?
- *Nonne lege hiemali ludimus?*

This is a gimme, isn't it?
- *Nonne hoc mihi datur?*

Isn't that lucky! My ball just rolled out of the rough and onto the fairway!
- *Fortunatus sum! Pila mea de gramine horrido modo in pratum lene recta volvit!*

On the Tennis Court

It's just out!
- *Paulo praeter regionem est!*

A little wide!
- *Minime latum!*

It was just a hair long!
- *Longius capillo fuit!*

It's out by an inch!
- *Una uncia abest!*

On the Slopes

Boy, I hate lift lines.
- *Heu, odi manere in agmine pro sellis volatilibus.*

Watch where you're going, you jerk!
- *Observa quo vadis, cinaede!*

Avalanche!
- *Lapsus nivium!*

Let's get in the hot tub!
- *In thermulas intremus!*

At the Beach

Look at the hooters on that one.
- *Ecce illa mammeata.*

Let's build a sand Forum.
- *Forum harenae aedificemus.*

Do you want a frosty one?
- *Visne frigidum?*

What's that in the water?
- *Quid est illud in aqua?*

Shark! Shark!
- *Pistrix! Pistrix!*

ON A YACHT

What happens if I pull this rope?
- *Quid fiat si hoc rudentem vellam?*

Can I drive?
- *Licetne mihi gubernare?*

Is there supposed to be a lot of water down here?
- *Debetne multum aquae subter esse?*

All of a sudden I'm not feeling so good.
- *Subito minime valeo.*

AT THE SPA

There is something wrong with this scale.
- *Haec trutina errat.*

Was your masseur trained in East Germany?
- *Tractatorne in Germania Orientali doctus est?*

It's on a plate, it must be food.
- *In catillo est, cibus esse debet.*

Is there an alcoholic beverage made from oat bran?
- *Estne ebriamen de furfure avenaceo factum?*

THINGS TO SAY TO YOUR LAWYER

Listen, would you repeat everything you just told me, only this time say it in English.
- *Heu, modo itera omnia quae mihi nunc nuper narravisti, sed nunc Anglice.*

You charge how much an hour?
- *Quantum in una hora imputas?*

THINGS TO SAY TO YOUR ACCOUNTANT

This amount here, is that what I made or what I owe?
- *Haec summa, estne quod merui aut quod debeo?*

Where do I sign?
- *Ubi signo?*

Things to Say to the IRS Agent

Unfortunately, I can't find those particular documents.
- *Eheu, litteras istas reperire non possum.*

I know why the numbers don't agree! I use Roman numerals!
- *Scio cur summae inter se dissentiant! Numeris Romanis utor!*

Things to Say to Your Banker

I don't want a toaster.
- *Furnulum pani nolo.*

I can't be overdrawn.
- *Fieri non potest ut ratio mea deficiat.*

Things to Say to Your Stockbroker

Just what exactly is a pork belly?
- *Quidnam est sterilicula?*

I thought the idea was to buy low and sell high.
- *Credidi pretio parvo emere et magno vendere tibi in animo fuisse.*

Are you telling me that sunspots caused the market crash?
- *Dicisne mihi maculas in sole mercatum labi fecisse?*

THINGS TO SAY TO YOUR DENTIST

This isn't going to hurt, is it?
- *Num mihi dolebit hoc?*

Something important came up, so I'll have to cancel my appointment.
- *Quadam re magna facta constitutum meum mihi deponendum est.*

THINGS TO SAY TO YOUR PSYCHIATRIST

Sometimes I get this urge to conquer large parts of Europe.
- *Interdum feror cupidine partium magnarum Europae vincendarum.*

I think some people in togas are plotting against me.
- *Sentio aliquos togatos contra me conspirare.*

I have this compulsion to speak Latin.
- *Latine loqui coactus sum.*

What has my mother got to do with it?
- *Quid agitur de matre mea?*

Things to Say to a Teenager

Really rad, dude!
- *Radicitus, comes!*

What's happening?
- *Quid fit?*

Things to Say to an Obnoxious Child

In the good old days, children like you were left to perish on windswept crags.
- *Antiquis temporibus, nati tibi similes in rupibus ventosissimis exponebantur ad necem.*

I'm rubber, you're glue, bounces off me, sticks to you!
- *Flexilis sum, gluten es, me resilit, ad te haeret!*

Things to Say to a Movie Star

You look shorter and older in person.
- *Videris humilior seniorque coram.*

Can I have your autograph?
- *Licetne tibi mihi dare tuam subscriptionem?*

Things to Say to the Hoi Polloi

I do not have any spare change.
- *Est mihi nullus nummus superfluus.*

I gave at the office.
- *In tabulario donationem feci.*

I do not wish to "check it out."
- *Nolo id "perscrutari."*

I'm not interested in your dopey religious cult.
- *Nihil curo de ista tua stulta superstitione.*

If Caesar were alive, you'd be chained to an oar.
- *Caesar si viveret, ad remum dareris.*

Things to Say to a Malfunctioning Soft-Drink Machine

You infernal machine! Give me a beverage or give me back my money!
- *Machina improba! Vel mihi ede potum vel mihi redde nummos meos!*

VI.
TACTICAL LATIN
Lingua Latina Rationi

EMBARRASSING SITUATIONS ARE LESS EMBARRASSING IN LATIN

I'd like to buy some condoms.
- *Volo comparare nonnulla tegumembra.*

I didn't expect you home so soon!
- *Non sperabam te domum tam cito revenire!*

I don't know how that got into my pocket.
- *Nescio quomodo illud in sinum meum intraverit.*

Of course I know what day today is! I just can't remember the English word for it.
- *Scilicet scio quid sit hodiernus dies! Modo ei non possum meminisse verbum Anglicum.*

Oh! I was just looking to see whether you had any Kleenex here among these papers on your desk.
- *O! Conabar cognoscere num tibi adsit Nascida in mensa tua inter haec scripta.*

Do you by any chance happen to own a large, yellowish, very flat cat?
- *Estne tibi forte magna feles fulva et planissima?*

Bald-Faced Lies Are Less Bald-Faced in Latin

The check is in the mail.
* *Perscriptio in manibus tabellariorum est.*

I have nothing to declare.
* *Nihil declaro.*

I don't know what you're talking about.
* *Nescio quid dicas.*

It was that way when I got here.
* *Ita erat quando hic adveni.*

There's no one here by that name.
* *Nemo hic adest illius nominis.*

Don't call me, I'll call you.
* *Noli me vocare, ego te vocabo.*

Flattery Sounds More Sincere in Latin

Have you lost weight?
* *Nonne macescis?*

You haven't aged a bit!
* *Minime senuisti!*

It looks great on you!
* *Id tibi praebet speciem lepidissimam!*

A wig? I never would have guessed!
* *Capillamentum? Haudquaquam conieci esse!*

INTIMATE SUBJECTS ARE EASIER TO BROACH IN LATIN

Your fly is open.
- *Braccae tuae aperiuntur.*

Your slip is showing.
- *Subucula tua apparet.*

You have a big piece of spinach on your front teeth.
- *In dentibus anticis frustum magnum spinaciae habes.*

You've been misusing the subjunctive.
- *Abutebaris modo subjunctivo.*

SELF-ASSERTIVENESS IS SIMPLER IN LATIN

Hey, we're all in line here!
- *Heus, hic nos omnes in agmine sunt!*

No cutting in!
- *Noli inferre se in agmen!*

No, excuse me, I believe *I'm* next.
- *Non, mihi ignosce, credo me insequentem esse.*

You're from New York, aren't you?
- *Nonne de Novo Eboraco venis?*

THREATS CARRY MORE WEIGHT IN LATIN

Watch out—you might end up divided into three parts, like Gaul.
- *Prospice tibi—ut Gallia, tu quoque in tres partes dividaris.*

People will soon be referring to you in the past pluperfect tense.
- *In tempore praeterito plus quam perfecto de te mox dicent.*

If I were you, I wouldn't walk in front of any catapults.
- *Cave ne ante ullas catapultas ambules.*

FIGHTING WORDS ARE SAFER IN LATIN

What did you call me?
- *Quid me appellavisti?*

Yeah, I'm talking to you.
- *Ita, te adloquor.*

You want to repeat that?
- *Visne illud iterare?*

A comedian, huh?
- *Ita vero, esne comoedus?*

Oh yeah? Your mother!
- *Itane? Tua mater!*

You want to make something of it?
- *Visne aliquid de illo facere?*

You and whose army?
- *Tutene? Atque cuius exercitus?*

Let's step outside.
- *Foras gradiamur.*

Well, if you don't understand plain Latin, I'm not going to dirty my hands on you.
- *Bene, cum Latine nescias, nolo manus meas in te maculare.*

Excuses Sound More Believable in Latin

My dog ate it.
- *Canis meus id comedit.*

The cleaning lady threw it away.
- *Ancilla id abiecit.*

It fell into the shredder.
- *Id in machinam schidarum scindendarum incedit.*

I did call. Maybe your answering machine is broken.
- *Sane ego te vocavi. Forsitan capedictum tuum desit.*

My watch stopped.
- *Horologium manuale meum stitit.*

My car wouldn't start.
- *Currus meus se movere noluit.*

I was kidnapped by aliens. What year is it?
- *Hostes alienigeni me abduxerunt. Qui annus est!*

B.S. Is More Convincing in Latin

I'm glad you asked me that.
- *Gaudeo te illud de me rogavisse.*

I'll put all my cards on the table.
- *Chartas meas omnes in tabulam ponam.*

You know, I'm your biggest fan.
- *Edepol, fautor tuus maximus sum.*

I'm only thinking of what's best for you.
- *Modo cogito quid prosit rebus tuis.*

Believe me, this hurts me more than it hurts you.
- *Mihi crede, hoc mihi magis quam tibi nocet.*

Latin Medical Names for Nonexistent But Useful Diseases

Impedimentum memoriae
- (A mental block that makes it hard for you to remember names)

Inopia celeritatis
- (A mild dyslexia that makes it impossible to arrive on time)

Dolor anteprandialis
- (A gastric problem that occasionally makes you cancel a lunch)

Morbus irrigationis
- (A rare disease aggravated by watering friends' plants)

Taedium pellucidorum
- (An eye condition that keeps you from looking at people's slides)

AN ALL-PURPOSE EVASION OF A REQUEST FOR A LATIN TRANSLATION

You can't say that in Latin.
- *Illud Latine dici non potest.*

AN ALL-PURPOSE PHONY TRANSLATION OF A LATIN INSCRIPTION

"Having done these things, they made the sacrifices prescribed by custom lest they be found lacking in filial piety."

VII.
CULTURAL LATIN
Lingua Latina Docta

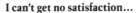

At the Theater

If you want good tickets, you've got to go to a scalper.
- *Si desideras tesseras bonas tibi opus est ad sectorem ire.*

You know, we really ought to go to the theater more often.
- *Pol, ad spectaculum saepius nobis eundum est.*

Fire!
- *Flamma!*

At a Concert

What time do you think we'll be out of here?
- *Quo tempore credis nos exituros?*

Is it over? Do I applaud now?
- *Estne confectum? Nuncine applaudo?*

At a Literary Gathering

Seen any good movies lately?
- *Vidistine nuper imagines moventes bonas?*

How about those Forty-Niners?
- *Quid sentis de Undequinquagintis?*

At a Poetry Reading

It doesn't rhyme.
- *Nullo metro compositum est.*

I don't care. If it doesn't rhyme, it isn't a poem.
- *Non curo. Si metrum non habet, non est poema.*

At an Art Exhibition

You call this art? A two-year-old could do better.
- *Dicisne hoc opus artem esse? Quivis infans rem meliorem facere potest.*

I don't know much about art, but I know what I like.
- *Cum Musis deditus non sim, nosco quod amo.*

AT THE VATICAN

Know where I can get a cup of coffee around here?
- *Scisne ubi pocillum coffeae apud hanc locum possim capere?*

Is this the way to the Sistine Chapel?
- *Ducitne haec via ad Capellam Sextinam?*

Is it all right if I use a flash in here?
- *Licetne mihi hic fulgure uteri?*

Now *that's* a ceiling!
- *Ecce lacunar mirum!*

Is this the only gift shop?
- *Haecine taberna munusculorum unica est?*

Excuse me, can you recommend a good restaurant nearby?
- *Nisi molestum est, potesne mihi recommendare popinam bonam vicinam?*

Where can I get a hat like that?
- *Ubi possum potiri petasi similis isti?*

AT THE MOVIES

This is a remake of a French film.
- *Haec imago movens ex pristina Gallicana recreata est.*

The sequel is never as good as the original.
- *Sequella numquam tam bona est quam origo.*

Look out, there's some crud on this seat.
- *Cave, aliquod squaloris est in hac sede.*

Timeless Lines from the Movies

Make my day.
- *Fac ut gaudeam.*

Round up the usual suspects.
- *Conlige suspectos semper habitos.*

You know, Toto, I have a feeling we're not in Kansas anymore.
- *Certe, Toto, sentio nos in Kansate non iam adesse.*

Frankly, my dear, I don't give a damn.
- *Re vera, cara mea, mea nil refert.*

All Music Is Classical Music in Latin

My favorite group is . . .
- *Caterva carissima mea est . . .*

The Beatles
Cimictus

The Temptations
Inlecebrae

The Rolling Stones
Lapides Provolventes

The Who
Ille Quis

The Grateful Dead
Mortui Grati

The Monkees
Simitatores

The Beach Boys
Pueri Litoris

Country Joe and the Fish
Iosephus Agrestis Piscesque

ALL TV IS EDUCATIONAL TV IN LATIN

My favorite show is . . .
• *Spectaculum carissimum est . . .*

Gilligan's Island
Insula Gilliganis

Hollywood Squares
Quadrata Iliceti

The Love Boat
Navis Amoris

Leave It to Beaver
Id Castori Concedite

Mission: Impossible
Opus: Quod Fieri Non Potest

Hawaii Five-O
Hawaii Quinque-Nil

The Gong Show
Spectaculum Tintinnabuli

The Price Is Right
Pretium Iustum Est

Jeopardy
Periculum

Wheel of Fortune
Rota Fortunae

Diff'rent Strokes
Ictus Diff'rentes

Happy Days
Dies Felices

The Young and the Restless
Iuvenes Inquietesque

Divorce Court
Curia Divortiorum

The Flintstones
Illi Silices

The Twilight Zone
Zona Crepusculi

VIII.
SOCIAL LATIN
Lingua Latina Vitae Communi

In a Bar

I'll have . . .
- *Da mihi sis . . .*

> . . . a light beer.
> . . . *cerevisiam dilutam.*

> . . . a glass of white wine.
> . . . *poculum vini albi.*

> . . . a martini.
> . . . *spiculum argenteum.*

> . . . a fog cutter.
> . . . *quod nebulam dissipat.*

I'll drink to that!
- *Hoc ei propinabo!*

Bartender! Another round!
- *Caupo! Etiamnunc!*

Cheers!
- *Propino tibi salutem!*

At a WASP Country Club

That is the largest drink I have ever seen.
- *Illa potio maxima est a me visa.*

I think several of the people here are dead.
- *Credo nonnullos hic mortuos esse.*

Those green pants go so well with that pink shirt and the
plaid jacket!
- *Braccae illae virides cum subucula rosea et tunica Caledonia—
quam eleganter concinnatur!*

I can't understand what you are saying. Are your jaws wired
together?
- *Verba tua intellegere non possum. Filone ferreo maxillae tuae
iunctae sunt?*

At a Hip Disco

Do you want to dance? I know the Funky Broadway.
- *Visne saltare? Viam Latam Fungosam scio.*

How do you get your hair to do that?
- *Quomodo cogis comas tuas sic videri?*

At a Birthday Party

Happy birthday!
- *Tibi diem natalem felicem!*

Here's a pinch to grow an inch!
- *Te vellico ut uncia crescas!*

Speech! Speech!
- *Ora! Ora!*

At a Family Reunion

Put on a little weight, haven't you?
- *Nonne aliquantulum pinguescis?*

Is that a gray hair?
- *Illaecine canities?*

Honey/buster, when are you going to get married?
- *Mellita/comes, quando aliquem/aliquam in matrimonium accipies/duces?*

You're not going to get a divorce, are you?
- *Num est tibi in animo divortium facere?*

Face it, you're stuck in a dead-end job.
- *Aspice, officio fungeris sine spe honoris amplioris. .*

Say, you sure are drinking a lot.
- *Re vera, potas bene.*

Isn't it great to have the whole family together?
- *Nonne dulce est familiam totam in unum locum cogere?*

At Your High School Reunion

Oh! Was I speaking Latin again?
- *Vah! Denuone Latine loquebar?*

Silly me. Sometimes it just sort of slips out.
- *Me ineptum. Interdum modo elabitur.*

Talking to Pets

Polly want a cracker?
- *Pulle! Visne frustum?*

Sit! Roll over! You see, he understands Latin.
- *Sede! Volve! Ecce, Latine scit.*

Bad kitty! Why don't you use the cat box? I put new litter in it.
- *Feles mala! Cur cista non uteris! Stramentum novum in ea posui.*

USEFUL CURSES

May barbarians invade your personal space!
- *Utinam barbari spatium proprium tuum invadant!*

May conspirators assassinate you in the mall!
- *Utinam coniurati te in foro interficiant!*

May faulty logic undermine your entire philosophy!
- *Utinam logica falsa tuam philosophiam totam suffodiant!*

May you always misuse the subjunctive!
- *Utinam modo subiunctivo semper male utaris!*

Biological Terms of Endearment

Homo sapiens
- A human being

Fiber fervidus
- An eager beaver

Cuniculus inscius
- A dumb bunny

Pavo absolutus
- A total turkey

Lacertus atrioli
- A lounge lizard

Fera festiva
- A party animal

Radix lecti
- A couch potato

IX.
SENSUAL LATIN
Lingua Latina Libidinosa

STARTING A RELATIONSHIP

Do you come here often?
- *Frequentasne hunc locum?*

Haven't we met somewhere before?
- *Nonne alicubi prius convenimus?*

What's your sign?
- *Quo signo nata es?*

You strike me as a very deep person.
- *Apparet te habere ingenium profundum.*

I feel that I already know you.
- *Sentio me iam te novisse.*

I think fate brought us together.
- *Credo fatum nos coegisse.*

Your place or mine?
- *Apudne te vel me?*

HAVING A RELATIONSHIP

You know, the Romans invented the art of love.
- *Romani quidem artem amatoriam invenerunt.*

A little more up and to the right.
- *Paululum sursum et dextrorsum.*

Oh! More! Go on! Yes! Ooh! Ummm!
- *O! Plus! Perge! Aio! Hui! Hem!*

ENDING THE RELATIONSHIP

Let's not rush into anything.
- *In ullam rem ne properemus.*

I'm not ready to make a commitment.
- *Non sum paratus me committere.*

I'm not sure we're right for each other.
- *Nescio num alius idoneus alii sit.*

I hope we'll still be friends.
- *Spero nos familiares mansuros.*

I guess fate wanted us to part.
- *Suspicor fatum nos voluisse diversos.*

X.
ASTRONOMICAL LATIN
Lingua Latina Cenatica

In a Fast-Food Restaurant

I'll have . . .
* *Da mihi sis . . .*

> . . . a hamburger, French fries, and a thick shake.
> . . . *bubulae frustum assae, solana tuberosa in modo Gallico fricta ac quassum lactatum coagulatum crassum.*

> . . . a bucket of fried chicken.
> . . . *hamam pulli tosti.*

> . . . a pizza with everything on it.
> . . . *crustum Etruscum cum omnibus in eo.*

In a Chain Theme Restaurant

I want the Buffalo chicken wings.
* *Alas gallinaceas de urbe Bovis volo.*

The waitress drew a smiley face on my check.
* *Ancilla in computatione faciem subridentem pinxit.*

At a Pretentious Restaurant

Frankly, I think the chef put too much thyme in the sauce.
- *Ut vere dicam, credo coquum nimium thymi in liquamen mississe.*

Look at the size of that pepper mill.
- *Ecce magnitudinem illae molae piperi.*

It's a nice little wine, but it lacks character and depth.
- *Vinum bellum iucundumque est, sed animo corporeque caret.*

In a Chinese Restaurant

Please, no MSG.
- *Parce, sodes, glutamato monosodio.*

Do you have "flied lice?" Ha ha ha.
- *Habesne "olyzam flictam?" Hae hae hae.*

At the Stop 'n' Shop

Look! . . .
* *Ecce!* . . .

. . . Jelly beans	. . . Potato chips
. . . *Fabae suaves*	. . . *Assulae solanorum tuberosorum*
. . . Gummy Bears	. . . Coca-Cola
. . . *Ursuli Gummi*	. . . *Cola-Coca*
. . . Bubble gum	. . . Cheez Whiz
. . . *Manducabulla*	. . . *Caseus Velox*
. . . Mars Bars	. . . Twinkies
. . . *Lateres Martiales*	. . . *Scintillae*
. . . Milky Ways	. . . Tinfoil
. . . *Viae Lacteae*	. . . *Bractea stannea*
. . . Moon Pies	. . . Glad Bags
. . . *Crusta Lunares*	. . . *Sacci Laeti*
. . . Pretzels	. . . Aspirin
. . . *Nodi salsi*	. . . *Pilulae acetylsalicylicae*

Things to Say While Barbecuing

Take a look at those steaks!
* *Contemplare carunculas illas!*

You've really got to soak the charcoal with fuel.
* *Necesse est carbonem igne Graeco madefacere.*

The mosquitoes are murder tonight!
* *Culices pessimi hac nocte sunt!*

Ever noticed how wherever you stand, the smoke goes right into your face?
* *Animadvertistine, ubicumque stes, fumum recta in faciem ferri!*

Come and get it!
* *Venite ac capite!*

A Roman Recipe

1. Get 1,000 larks.
2. Remove their tongues and set aside.
3. Discard the larks.
4. Put the tongues in a pan with a little oil and sauté quickly.
5. Transfer to a hot platter. Serves four.

I. *Alaudarum* M *cape.*
II. *Linguas exseca et sepone.*

III. *Alaudas abice.*
IV. *Linguas mitte in sartaginem cum paulo olei et frige cito.*
V. *Eas traice ad patellam calidam. Quattuor sufficit.*

Domestic Discourse

Honey, I'm home.
- *Mellita, domi adsum.*

Sheesh, what a day!
- *Mehercle, qui dies!*

You did what to the car?
- *Quid carrus passus est?*

You paid how much for that dress?
- *Quantum illae stolae pependisti?*

Something's burning.
- *Aliquid ardet.*

Oh, no, it's the roast, and the boss is coming to dinner!
- *Vae, ardet assa bubula atque patronus ad cenam veniet!*

MINOR MISUNDERSTANDINGS

Shopping list? What shopping list?
- *Libellus comparandorum? Qui libellus comparandorum?*

I thought you were going to pick up the kids.
- *Credidi te liberos colligere.*

Don't ask me where the keys are. You had them last.
- *Noli me rogare ubi sint claves. Eas nunc nuper habebas.*

But you told me your mother was coming *next* month!
- *Sed me docuisti matrem tuam* postero *mense venturam esse!*

A call from someone named "Bubbles?" It's a wrong number.
- *Vocatusne de quadam "Bullula" nomine? Numerus falsus est.*

TABLE TALK

My favorite! Tuna-noodle casserole!
- *Mea dilectissima! Farrago thunni!*

What do you say we join the clean-plate club.
- *Nos coniungamus collegio patellae purae.*

You'll eat it and like it, or you'll have it for breakfast tomorrow.
- *Aut id devorabis amabisque, aut cras prandebis.*

Don't play with your food! Remember the starving Carthaginians!
- *Noli ludere alimento! Memento Carthaginienses esurientes!*

LAYING DOWN THE LAW

This report card is a disgrace.
- *Haec renuntatio infamis est.*

Pay attention! I'm speaking to you!
- *Ausculta mihi! Tibi dico!*

You're grounded!
- *Ad domum adligaris!*

No TV for a week!
- *Nullam ultravisionem spectabis per septem dies!*

I'm cutting your allowance in half!
- *Peculium dimidiatum est!*

When I was your age . . .
- *Cum tam iuvenis eram quam nunc es . . .*

> . . . I had a full-time job in a salt mine.
> . . . *in salinis diu laborabam.*

> . . . I won the Nobel Prize for promptness and neatness.
> . . . *Praemium Nobelium celeritatis et munditiae abstuli.*

> . . . I could speak Latin.
> . . . *Latine loqui poteram.*

Tough Talk

N-O spells *No!*
- *Verbum non N.O.N. scribitur!*

Nothing doing, and that's final.
- *Haud fiet, et clavo fixum est.*

I don't care what the other parents are doing.
- *Curae mihi non est quod alii parentes faciant.*

I am not being unreasonable.
- *Non sum iniquus.*

All right, we'll ask your mother.
- *Bene, matrem tuam rogabimus.*

Okay, just this once.
- *Ita, semel et solum tibi permissum est.*

Discussing the Baby-Sitter

I think she's from another planet.
- *Arbitror eam de planeta alia venisse.*

Did her parents drop her off here in a spacecraft?
- *Astroscaphane parentes eam huc portaverunt!*

Maybe she's just a drug addict.
- *Fortasse modo opio addicta est.*

I think I've seen her face on a milk carton or down at the post office.
- *Credo me faciem suam in olla lactis vel in tabulario tabellariorum vidisse.*

In the Men's Department

This suit looks a little baggy.
- *Vestimentum laxum paululum videtur.*

The lapels are too wide.
- *Fimbriae latiores sunt.*

I don't like this shade.
- *Colorem hunc non diligo.*

Honey, what do you think?
- *Mellilla, quid sentis?*

When will it be ready?
- *Quando praesto fiet?*

ON THE ROAD

We ought to have made that turn.
- *Nos opertuit tunc vertisse.*

Give me the map.
- *Mihi da tabulam.*

Let's ask directions.
- *Aliquem de via consulamus.*

Would you like me to drive?
- *Visne me currum agere?*

I am *not* lost.
- *Neutiquam erro.*

Settle down back there.
- *Sedate vos, posteriores.*

Why didn't you go when you had the chance?
- *Cur non isti mictum ex occasione?*

You'll just have to hold it in.
- *Opus est tibi urinam inhibere.*

Next time you'll take the bus.
- *Carro Canis Cani veharis posthac.*

At a Black-Tie Dinner Party

Let's switch place cards.
- *Chartas loci mutemus.*

Is this the right fork?
- *Hacine furcilla uti decet?*

Wait, that's my bread plate.
- *Siste, patella panis est mea.*

Do I drink this or stick my fingers in it?
- *Hocine bibo aut in eum digitos insero?*

My dessert is on fire!
- *Mensa secunda mea flagrat!*

AT A WEDDING

It's not too late to back out!
- *Non serus matrimonium fugias.*

AT A CHRISTENING

Do you ever worry that there was a mix-up at the hospital?
- *Vobisne curae umquam est num in valetudinario confusio facta sit?*

AT A FUNERAL

Remember when we only used to run into each other at weddings?
- *Meministine cum nos solum in nuptiis obviam eramus?*

FINAL LATIN

DENIQUE DIAETAM EFFICACEM INVENI
- AT LAST I HAVE FOUND A DIET THAT WORKS

NUNC, VERO INTER SAXUM ET LOCUM DURUM SUM
- NOW, I REALLY AM BETWEEN A ROCK AND A HARD PLACE

DIXI ME AEGROTARE, SED ECQUIS AUSCULTARET?
- I SAID I WAS SICK, BUT WOULD ANYBODY LISTEN?

TAM EXANIMIS QUAM TUNICA NEHRU FIO
- I AM AS DEAD AS THE NEHRU JACKET

INVICEM, RES BONA EST NON PLUS DENTHARPAGARUM
- ON THE OTHER HAND, THE GOOD NEWS IS NO MORE DENTISTRY

SIC FRIATUR CRUSTUM DULCE
- IT IS THUS THAT THE COOKIE CRUMBLES

OBESA CANTAVIT
- THE FAT LADY HAS SUNG

LATIN
FOR EVEN MORE
OCCASIONS

*Lingua Latina
Multo Pluribus Occasionibus*

Oh, darn, there I go again! You know, I just can't help speaking Latin.

Ecce, denuo ago, sicut soleo! Non enim possum facere quin Latine loquar.

It's so second nature to me, sometimes I don't even know I'm doing it!

Adeo huius mihi rei natura facta est, ut interdum nesciam quidem me sic facere!

PREFACE

Praefatio

As you can tell from the title of this book, *Lingua Latina Multo Pluribus Occasionibus* (Latin for Even More Occasions) is a sequel. It was written as a companion volume to *Lingua Latina Occasionibus Omnibus* (Latin for All Occasions), but it is also a complete work in its own right, containing hundreds of all-new translations of everyday English expressions into grammatically accurate, idiomatically correct classical Latin, and incorporating the same foolproof, easy-to-use Latin pronunciation guide found in its predecessor.

Now, even though the word "sequel" comes directly from Latin (you probably spotted it right away as a derivative of the third-conjugation deponent verb *sequor, sequi, secutus sum*: to follow) and even though the *Aeneid*, Virgil's precedent-setting epic poem, has *twelve* books, the fact is, we never planned to produce a follow-up to our original collection of handy conversational Latin phrases.

Frankly, the reason why we chose a sweeping title like *Lingua Latina Occasionibus Omnibus* (Latin for All Occasions) in the first place, instead of something safer like *Iam Ardebat Cum Citheram Meam Sustuli* (It Was On Fire When I Picked Up My Fiddle) was that we truly felt that the book had not only thoroughly covered the territory in question, but had looted it, subjugated it, and built a pretty impressive system of roads and aqueducts across it.

Well, *peccavimus* (we goofed). Even though our *magnum opus* (magnum opus) included everything from cocktail-party chitchat and singles-bar banter to high-powered business buzzwords and Hollywood mogul jargon, the many letters we've received since its publication from readers seeking the precise translation of a phrase that wasn't in the book but was right on the tips of their tongues (in some cases, the lines in question occupied their entire tongue surfaces) soon convinced us that more work remained to be done.

How, they wanted to know, do you say "Please don't squeeze the Charmin"? Should it have the polite *Noli* and an infinitive, or the poetic *Ne* and an imperative? When you croon "You Can't Always Get What You Want" in the shower, do you have to vocalize in the subjunctive? Can you say "I'm a rambling wreck from Georgia Tech" without using a gerund?

We also had numerous requests from people who needed a little assistance with Latin composition for specific purposes we hadn't thought of: like a brief after-dinner speech in the language of Cicero for those annoying occasions when some complete *podex* (aggravating person) calls upon you to make a few impromptu remarks; or a two-minute comedy routine worthy of Plautus so you can use a dead language to become the life of the party; or a bit of lighthearted infield chatter from the Campus Martius to unnerve the opposition in a friendly softball game.

Needless to say, we quickly realized that we had not only the opportunity, but also the obligation, to produce a second compendium of impeccably accurate Roman chin music to help those many classically trained individuals whose Latin is just a little rusty to "chew the toga" with absolute confidence. And of course it was that very real sense of duty, and not some cynical desire to *"lucrifacere"* ("cash in") on an improbable fad that we inadvertently created, that led to *Lingua Latina Multo Pluribus Occasionibus* (Latin for Even More Occasions).

At this point, some *mentula* (difficult individual) might be tempted to ask, "So, is this series going to have a third part someday?"

Really. Of all the Gaul.

Salvete ('Bye) and *Die dulci fruimini* (Have a nice day)!

ACKNOWLEDGMENTS
Gratiae

I would like to thank Mark Sugars, who not only corrected the many inflectional errors and grammatical inaccuracies in my manuscript but also suggested countless changes, both large and small, which have conferred on this book a degree of classical polish and linguistic refinement that I could never have produced on my own. If there are any laurels handed out for a particularly well chosen phrase or elegant piece of diction, his brow is the appropriate repository for the honorary vegetation. If, on the other hand, there are any howlingly infelicitous constructions or outright boo-boos, the dunce cap belongs on my noggin.

I would also like to note for the record, now that the success of *Lingua Latina Occasionibus Omnibus* (Latin for All Occasions) makes it clear that I am engaging in a sincere effort to share the credit rather than a transparent attempt to shift the blame, that the idea for these books was entirely John Boswell's, as was the overall concept for their format. And I'd also like to express our gratitude to Peter Gethers, whose bold (some might say foolhardy) decision to publish a collection of conversational Latin phrases makes Hannibal's crossing of the Alps by elephant seem by comparison a pretty ho-hum pachyderm deployment.

H.B.

CONTENTS
Quod in Libro Continetur

I.
CASUAL LATIN
Lingua Latina Quotidiana

FRENCH SOUNDS EVEN BETTER IN LATIN

Savoir faire
- *Scire facere*

Déjà vu
- *Prius visum*

Nouveau riche
- *Novissime locupletatus*

Joie de vivre
- *Gaudium vivendi*

De rigueur
- *Coactus*

Tête-à-tête
- *Capitibus conlatis*

Comme ci, comme ça
- *Medio, modico*

Plus ça change, plus c'est la même chose
- *Quo magis mutat, eo magis perstat*

Merde!
- *Merda!*

Latin: It's More Than a Language—It's an Attitude

Yes, I have a personal Latin trainer.
- *Aio, exercitorem linguae Latinae proprium habeo.*

We're working on my ablatives and subjunctives.
- *Exercemus casus ablativos et modos subjunctivos meos.*

I want to get my syntax into shape for the beach this summer.
- *Volo ut syntaxis mea splendescat in litore, veniente aestate.*

The Basic Philosophies Are Best Expressed in Latin

I think, therefore I am.
- *Cogito, ergo sum.*

I am, therefore I eat.
- *Sum, ergo edo.*

I think, therefore I am depressed.
- *Cogito, ergo doleo.*

I think I'll have another drink.
- *Cogito sumere potum alterum.*

ALL BOOKS ARE GREAT BOOKS IN LATIN

Glitter
- *Fulgor*

Princess Daisy
- *Regis Filia Composita*

Valley of the Dolls
- *Valles Puparum*

Once Is Not Enough
- *Semel Non Satis Est*

Smart Women, Foolish Choices
- *Mulieres Sapientes, Optiones Ineptae*

Living, Loving, and Learning
- *Vivere, Amare, Discere*

I'm OK—You're OK
- *Valeo—Vales*

Everything You Always Wanted to Know About Sex but Were Afraid to Ask
- *Omnia Quae De Sexu Cognoscere Semper Voluisti sed Rogare Metuisti*

Snippets of Poetry Are Easier to Wedge into the Conversation in Latin

A rose is a rose is a rose.
- *Rosa rosa rosa est est.*

Do I dare to eat a peach?
- *Audeone persicum edere?*

Not with a bang but a whimper
- *Non crepitu, sed vagitu*

And quoth the Raven, "Nevermore!"
- *Ac dixit Corvus, "Numquam postea!"*

Dopey Exhortations Are More Forceful in Latin

Go with the flow.
- *Ventis secundis, tene cursum.*

Don't let the bastards wear you down.
- *Noli nothis permittere te terere.*

Lead, follow, or get out of the way.
- *Duc, sequere, aut de via decede.*

Let it all hang out.
- *Totum dependeat.*

THERE IS NO SUCH THING AS A STUPID QUESTION IN LATIN

What, in a nutshell, is deconstructionism?
- *Paucis verbis, quid est deconstructionismus?*

Who exactly are the Kurds?
- *Quinam sunt Carduchi?*

Wouldn't nuclear winter cancel out the greenhouse effect?
- *Nonne hiems, quae incendiis magnis multisque belli inter gentes omnes tertii inducatur, inhibeat orbem terrarum ne nimium calescat?*

If you put a little pyramid on top, does that make something postmodern?
- *Si in culmine pyramidem parvam superponas, ita fit postnovitas?*

Your Two Cents' Worth Goes a Lot Farther in Latin

I'd much rather have a '55 Thunderbird than a '58 Corvette.
* *Magnopere malim Tonitravem anni MCMLV quam Corvettam anni MCMLVIII.*

Ali could have beaten Tyson.
* *Ali Tysonem vicisset, si pugnavissent.*

You really shouldn't keep a dog in the city.
* *Canis in urbe custodiendus non est.*

All frozen pizzas taste lousy.
* *Omnes lagani pistrinae gelati male sapiunt.*

You can't get a decent sound system for under a grand.
* *Non potes composituram machinarum quae apte musicam faciunt emere minoris quam mille.*

Things to Say to the Maître D' When You Don't Have a Reservation

Could you check again? My name must be there.
- *Inspice, sodes, denuo. Certo scio nomen adesse.*

I don't understand. My secretary called a week ago.
- *Non intellego. Scriba mea tibi filo dixit septem diebus ante.*

Listen, I have a very important business client with me.
- *Audi, mecum habeo socium in negotiis magni momenti.*

He's also my oldest friend.
- *Insuper etiam est amicus veterrimus.*

It's both of our birthdays.
- *Haec est nobis ambobus dies natalis.*

I'm a restaurant reviewer.
- *Cauponas percenseo.*

Here's ten bucks.
- *Ecce, tibi do decem denarium.*

Pretty please with cherry on top!
- *Te precor dulcissime supplex!*

LAS VEGAS LATIN

Are these slots progressive?
- *Crescuntne gradatim praedae ab his latronibus unibrachiis!*

I hit the jackpot!
- *Copiam cepi!*

Come on, baby needs a new pair of shoes!
- *Age, infanti opus est pari novorum calceorum!*

Damn! Snake eyes!
- *Vae! Canes!*

A fresh deck please, and cut 'em thin to win!
- *Sis, fer sarcinam recentem chartularum, et parti illas impariter ut praedas paremus!*

LATIN FOR THE LOTTERY

Do you have any tickets with Roman numerals?
- *Habesne ullas tesseras numeris Romanis impressas!*

No wonder I never win!
- *Non miror me numquam vicisse!*

LATIN: THE PERFECT PREPPY PATOIS

Let's mix up a pitcher of Bloodys, get crocked, and drop trou!
- *In urceo numerum Sanguineorum misceamus, ebrii fiamus, et bracas demittamus!*

Excellent! Intense quaffing action!
- *Praestantem! Nunc est adsiduo perpotandum!*

Major party bore! Biff's going to toss his tacos!
- *Taedium convivii maius! Byphis vomiturus est!*

He has to drive the big white bus to Woof City!
- *Sibi necesse est agere magnam raedam albam ad Municipium Eiectamenti!*

Let's bolt!
- *Evolemus!*

We're golden!
- *Aurei sumus!*

Aurelian Wall Street Latin

Greed is good.
- *Avaritia bona est.*

The name of the game is leverage.
- *Lusus cum pecunia mutua sumpta tibi ludendus est.*

I am a Master of the Universe!
- *Magister Mundi sum!*

I'm taking the Fifth!
- *Cito Emendationem Quintam!*

Latin: The Ultimate Yuppie Lingo

My Rolex is waterproof to twelve hundred meters.
- *Rolex meum vim aquae potest resistere usque ad altitudinem trium milium septingentorum pedum.*

I have a fax machine in my BMW.
- *In curro meo ab Officina Baiuoaria Mechanica fabricato habeo machinam quae litteras per aethera transmittit.*

I know a restaurant with only one table.
- *Novi cauponam quae solum unam mensam habet.*

My jogging suit is by Armani.
- *Armanius tunicam meam, quae apta est currendo, fecit.*

My Jacuzzi is filled with Perrier.
- *Meum balineum calidum verticosum cum aqua scintillante fontana Gallica impletum est.*

My bankruptcy lawyer is Alan Dershowitz.
- *Ego decoctor iuris consulto Alano Dershowitzi utor.*

HACKER LATIN: THE USER-FRIENDLY COMPUTER LANGUAGE

How's hacking, chiphead?
- *Quid agis, caput assulae?*

My motherboard fried! I am in a pessimal mode!
- *Tabula materna combusta est! Sum in modo pessimo!*

Some bagbiting technoweenie put a hungus Trojan horse in my program! It is munged!
- *Artifex plumipes qui merdam manducat in meo libello electronico qui regit computatorem equum Troianum posuit! Pessum datum est!*

I am globally torqued! Moby bogosity!
- *Funditus tortus sum! Fucatissimum!*

GOLDEN-AGE LATIN FOR NEW-AGE PEOPLE

Pyramids are out. I'm putting all my crystals in a little domed box shaped like the Pantheon.

- *Pyramides obsoletae sunt. Servo omnes gemmas crystallinas meas in cista formata in tholum instar Pantheonis.*

Using the subjunctive generates more alpha waves than meditation.

- *Modus subiunctivus gignit plus fluctuum alpha quam meditatio.*

Obviously your id, ego, and libido are going to be able to express themselves more fully in their native language—Latin.

- *Manifesto id, ego, et libido poterunt plenius se declarare lingua indigena—Latina videlicet.*

Roman numerology is a thousand years older than any Johnny-come-lately systems based on Arabic squiggles.

- *Vaticinatio quae numeris Romanis utitur vetustior est milibus annis quam ulla ratio sera quae scriptis Arabicis utitur.*

Om!

- *Omo, omas, omat, omamus, omatus, omant!*

LATIN IS ALWAYS POLITICALLY CORRECT

I sing of arms and a dead white male.
- *Arma virumque flavum atque mortuum cano.*

I came, I saw, I spoke out on a number of critical Third World issues.
- *Veni, vidi, verba feci de pluribus gravibus pertinentibus ad Partem Tertiam Orbis Terrarum, quae, ut scis, in partes tres divisa est.*

Languages that don't have separate genders are sexist!
- *Linguae quae genera distincta non habent inuriam faciunt feminis!*

Let us firmly reject all commands, conditions, and prohibitions that are not expressed in the subjunctive!
- *Repudiemus obstinate omnia mandata et condiciones et interdicta quae in modo subiunctivo non expressa sint!*

TIBER VALLEY GIRL

I'm, you know, in the mall, and I'm like talking to this major
    studmuffin?
- *Sum enim in foro, et modo, en, loquor cum quodam Adonide
    mero?*

It was totally awesome—I mean, really copious rad!
- *Omnino mirabile fuit—volo dicere, vero probe radicitus!*

And then I had negative clues, and I misused the subjunctive.
- *Tum autem indicia mihi erant obscura, et modo subiunctivo
    abusa sum.*

What a buzzstomp! Multiple sadness! I was mega raked!
- *O stridorem conculcatorum! Maestiam multiplicatam! Mag-
    nopere excruciata sum!*

Gag me with a spoon!
- *Fac me cocleario vomere!*

Funny, You Don't Look Latinish

Oy vay, what a—
• *Eheu, qualem—*

>> klutz!
>> *inhabilem!*
>>
>> schnook!
>> *blennum!*
>>
>> schlemiel!
>> *virum laevum!*
>>
>> yenta!
>> *oblatratricem!*
>>
>> gonif!
>> *furem!*
>>
>> schnorrer!
>> *parasitum!*
>>
>> kibitzer!
>> *interpellatorem!*
>>
>> nebbish!
>> *tenuiculum!*
>>
>> putz!
>> *verpam!*
>>
>> momser!
>> *nothum!*
>>
>> schmuck!
>> *mentulam!*

CHARIOTS OF THE ROMANS?

Okay, so if Plautus didn't write Shakespeare's plays, how
  come so many of them are set in Italy?
- *Ne scripserit Plautus Shakespearii fabulas, quamobrem tot ac-
  tae sunt utentes scaena Italica!*

Did you ever ask yourself why all the craters on the moon
  have *Latin* names?
- *Rogavistine umquam te ipsum cur sint omnibus crateribus in
  luna nomina* Latina!

Atlantis—Atlantic City. Think about it.
- *Atlantis—Urbs Atlantica. Cogita de hoc.*

Punch Lines Have More Punch in Latin

I can't hear you. I have a banana in my ear.
- *Te audire non possum. Musa sapientum fixa est in aure.*

You know, that dog isn't really all *that* shaggy.
- *Re vera, canis ille nequaquam* adeo *pilosus est.*

And at these prices, you won't see many more **kangaroos** in this bar, either.
- *Et tantis pretiis constitutis plures Macropodidas in hac caupona minime videbis.*

Wisecracks Are Wiser in Latin

Is that a scroll in your toga, or are you just happy to see me?
- *Estne volumen in toga, an solum tibi libet me videre?*

Take a picture, it lasts longer!
- *Fac imaginem, diutius durabit!*

ANYONE CAN DO A GREAT IMPRESSION—IN LATIN

JAMES CAGNEY
You dirty rat!
• *Tu, rattus turpis!*

MARLON BRANDO
I could've been a contender.
• *Proeliator fuissem.*

Make him an offer he can't refuse.
• *Ei fer condicionem quam non potest repudiare.*

CLINT EASTWOOD
Go ahead. Make my day.
• *Age. Fac ut gaudeam.*

CARY GRANT
Judy, Judy, Judy.
• *Iudaea, Iudaea, Iudaea.*

W. C. FIELDS
It was a woman who drove me to drink. I never stopped to thank her.
• *Fuit mulier quae me potare egit. Nunquam steti gradum ad ei gratias agendas.*

GROUCHO
I like my cigar, too, but I take it out of my mouth once in a while.
• *Fasciculum nicotianum fumificum meum quoque amo, sed aliquando eum de ore extraho.*

MAE WEST

Come up and see me sometime.

• *Interdum ascende ut me visas.*

LAUREN BACALL

You know how to whistle, don't you? Just put your lips
    together and blow.

• *Nonne scis sibilare? Labris compositis, perfla.*

BETTE DAVIS

What a dump!

• *Quid gurgustium!*

COMEDY NIGHT AT CAESAR'S PALACE

Take my wife, please!
- *Prehende uxorem meam, sis!*

No, but seriously . . .
- *Immo vero, serio . . .*

I just flew in from Gaul—boy, are my arms tired!
- *Nuperrime de Gallia huc volavi—Mehercle, bracchia mea defatigata sunt!*

Anyone here from Rome?
- *Adestne quisquam de Roma?*

Listen: I just got the latest score from the Colosseum—Lions 32, Christians 0, in sudden-death overtime!
- *Audite: Modo de Colosseo rationem interfectorum recentissimam cognovi—Leonibus triginta duo, Christianis nihil, clepsydra addita ad spatium mortis subitae!*

Do you know how many barbarians it takes to light a torch? One million—one to hold the torch, and the rest to get together and try to discover fire!
- *Scitisne quantus numerus barbarorum satis est ut ipsi facem accendere possint? Decies centena milia—uno facem tenente, debent ceteri convenire atque conari ignem invenire!*

You're just like my agent—you get ten percent of my jokes!
- *Simillimi procuratoris mei estis—iocorum meorum partem decimam prehenditis!*

But really, you've been a beautiful audience! I love ya, I love ya!
- *Sed vere, spectatores pulchri fuistis! Vos amo! Vos amo!*

A Sidesplitting Latin Telephone Answering-Machine Prank

FIRST CALL:
This is the Vatican calling for the pope. We need a ruling on a venial sin.
- *Hoc est Vaticanum. Pontificem maximum filo vocamus. Nobis opus est arbitrio de peccato veniale.*

SECOND CALL:
This is the College of Cardinals calling for the pope. We hope you can make it to the tailgate party next Saturday.
- *Hoc est Conlegium Cardinalium pontificem maximum filo vocans. Speramus te venturus esse ad convivium in tergis raedarum die Saturni proxima.*

THIRD CALL:
This is the caretaker at Castel Gondolfo. Your Holiness, do you want me to prune these olive trees?
- *Hic est custos Castelli Gondolfi. Papa Sanctissime, visne ut illas oleas putem?*

FOURTH CALL:
Hi, this is the pope. Have there been any messages for me?
- *Ave, hic est pontifex maximus qui tibi filo dicit. Mihine nuntia ulla fuerunt?*

A Latin Tongue Twister

How much wood would a woodchuck chuck if a woodchuck
could chuck wood?
- *Quantum materiae materietur marmota monax si marmota
  monax materiam possit materiari?*

Just as much wood as a woodchuck would if a woodchuck
could chuck wood.
- *Tantum materiae quam materietur marmota monax si marmota
  monax materiam possit materiari.*

Things to Say at a Toga Party

Are you wearing anything under that sheet?
- *Ullamne subuculam geris?*

Toga! Toga! Toga!
- *Togam! Togam! Togam!*

An All-Purpose Wedding Toast

I'd like to propose a toast to the happy couple and their
incompatability: His *income*, and her *pat-ability*!
- *Ego coniugibus felicibus propino: Scin quam inter se diversitas
  sit? Is* dives, *ea* versuta *est!*

An All-Purpose Latin After-Dinner Speech

You all probably think I am going to say something weighty
and memorable in Latin. Well, I'm not. What I'm going
to do is read you my laundry list. Here it is. Three pairs
of socks, five underwear, two shirts, no starch. There,
that's it. You can applaud now. Have a nice day.

- *Vos omnes fortasse creditis me aliquid grave ac memorabile
Latine dicturum esse. Re vera, illud facere non in animo habeo. Etenim perlecturus sum vobis catalogum lavandariorum.
Hic incipit. Tibialium paria tria, subuncularum quinque, tun-
icae duae, nullum amylum. Sic, actum est. Mihi plaudere nunc
potestis. Die dulci fruimini.*

AT THE AIRPORT

How long will the flight be delayed?
- *Quanta mora volatui fiet?*

What do you mean, you're overbooked?
- *Ain, supra modum sedes conductae sunt?*

Is there a way to get there without going through Atlanta?
- *Potestne illuc pervenire Atlantam tamen praeteriens?*

Do I get frequent-flier miles for the walk between gates?
- *Daturne praemium plurima milia passuum volandi mihi tantum spatium gresso inter portas?*

How about an upgrade?
- *Velisne me extollere ad cursum pretiosiorem?*

Stand aside, plebians! I am on imperial business!
- *Recedite, plebes! Gero rem imperialem!*

ON AN AIRPLANE

Will this seat go back any further?
- *Haecine sedes potest ultro reclinari?*

No, I don't want a red-hot towelette.
- *Minime! Nolo mantele candens.*

Is *Pet Health* the only magazine you have?
- *Estne* Valetudo Animalium Domesticorum *periodicus libellus solus quem ad manum habes?*

What is the movie on this flight?
- *Quis est cinematographia in hoc volatu?*

And you expect me to pay for the headphones?
- *Et credisne me empturum esse conchas soniferas?*

I'll have a Bloody Mary, please.
- *Velim sumere Mariam Sanguinariam, sis.*

Could you get that baby to shut up?
- *Potesne compescere ululatum istius infantis?*

Don't you have anything besides Salisbury Steak and Chicken Cacciatore?
- *Nonne alium cibum habes praeter Bubulam Sorbiodunensem et Pullum Coctum Modo Venatoris?*

Hey, you've been in there for twenty minutes.
- *Heia, viginti iam minutos in latrina ines.*

Yeah, it was a great flight. Now where do I go to get branded and have my hooves dipped?
- *Sic, volatus praestat. Nunc quo vadam ut nota in me inuratur et ungulae medicamentis mergantur?*

At the Rental-Car Counter

I don't want a subcompact.
- *Nolo cisium exiguum.*

I reserved a midsize.
- *Currum medium conduxi.*

Does this insurance cover me if I get sideswiped by some bastard in a chariot with knives on its wheels?
- *Subveniatne mihi haec fides damni resarciendi interposita si deiciar a nescio quo furcifero agente currum armatum defixis ad rotas cultris?*

Things to Say on a Cruise Ship

I hate shuffleboard.
- *Ludum tabulaticum odi.*

What time is lunch?
- *Quando prandimus?*

Hey, Captain, why don't you open her up and see what this baby can do?
- *Agedum, Magister, habenas dans monstra quam velociter hic phaselus currere possit!*

How do you say "Man overboard!" in English?
- *Quomodo dicitur Anglice "Vir in mare excidit!"?*

Are we sinking?
- *Summergimurne?*

Women, children, and Latin speakers first!
- *Feminae, infantes atque illi qui Latine loqui possint antecedant!*

MAKING NEW FRIENDS IN FOREIGN LANDS

SOUTH OF THE BORDER:
How come no one here speaks Latin? This is Latin America, isn't it?
- *Quapropter non adsunt qui Latine loquantur? Nonne est haec America Latina?*

ENGLAND:
Yeah? Well, how's *your* empire doing these days, smarty-pants?
- *Sic? Quomodonam se habet hodiernis diebus imperium tuum, salse bracate?*

FRANCE:
You know, you're not really speaking good French yourself—you're just badly mispronouncing lower-class provincial Latin.
- *Vero, tute reapse non bene loqueris Gallice—immo vero modo male et corrupte pronuntias sermonem Latinum plebium ac vernaculum.*

GERMANY:
So, who have you guys got lined up for your next world war?
- *Quos populos habetis in animo debellare proximo bello inter omnes gentes?*

ITALY:
Sheesh, have you let this place go downhill in the last two thousand years!
- *Mehercle, quantum sivistis hunc locum squalere annis proximis duobus milibus!*

SPAIN:

Look, why don't you throw a few Christians in there and let the bull win once in a while?

- *Ecce, inmitte sis in amphitheatrum paucos Christianos et permitte tauro aliquando vincere.*

AUSTRALIA:

G'day, mate. Will you please put another shrimp on the barbie for me?

- *Salve, socie. Pone mihi, sodes, alteram locustam marinam in caminello.*

Things to Say on the Orient Express

Quick, pretend you know me!
- *Cito, simula me cognoscere!*

See that man? He's a spy for the German tribes.
- *Videsne illum? Explorator Germanicus est.*

I have the plans for the new multiple independently targeted, boulder-hurling catapult. *Shhh!*
- *Descriptiones habeo catapultae novae quae saxos multos separatim et simul iaciant. St!*

If he gets his hands on them, it will be the end of the world as we know it.
- *Si illas prehendat, sit finis terrae qualem cognovimus.*

So, where are you headed?
- *Quo vadis?*

Things to Say in a Sidewalk Café

How are we to know whether we actually exist or only *think* we exist?
- *Quemadmodum possumus scire utrum vere simus an solum sentiamus nos esse?*

Can we ever truly distinguish art qua art from that which is merely pleasing to the eye?
- *Possumusne umquam vero artem ipsam secernere ab illis quae modo oculis grata sint?*

Could I get another cup of this great cappuccino and one of those little chocolate pastries?
- *Da mihi, sodes, alterum poculum huius capucincti suavissimi et unum e crustulis illis theobromaticis.*

You Sound Less Like a Tourist When You Gawk in Latin

Boy, if these old walls could talk!
- *Edepol, utinam hi parietes veteres dicere possint!*

How much do you think a painting like that would set you back?
- *Quanto credis picturam illius notae tibi staturam?*

If you sit on one of those chairs with a little rope across it, do you get a shock?
- *Si quis in unam ex illis sedibus, quibus funiculus est impositus, adsidat, cadat quasi fulmine stratus?*

That's the biggest bed I've ever seen.
- *Ille lectus est quem maximum vidi.*

How would you like to have a layout like this?
- *Nonne velis possidere latifundium similem huius?*

You could put a satellite dish on that turret.
- *Possis, si velis, in illa turricula ponere lancem ad stellas mechanicas auscultandas.*

There's enough room here for an eighteen-hole golf course.
- *Hic satis est spatium cursui ludi paganici Caledonii foraminum duodeviginti.*

But I bet the taxes and upkeep are murder.
- *Sed reor exactiones et impensas mortiferas esse.*

I wonder where the gift shop is.
- *Scire velim ubi taberna munusculorum sit.*

FOOD FOR THOUGHT: ROMANCE LANGUAGE MENU ALERT

horse	*caballus*
goat	*capra*
rabbit	*cuniculus*
brains	*cerebelli*
eel	*anguilla*
sea eels	*congri*
sea snails	*bucina*
sea slugs	*limaces*
lampreys	*lampredae*

V.
CONFIDENTIAL LATIN
Lingua Latina Sub Rosa

Latin Is Always Acceptable in Polite Company

Who cut the cheese?
- *Quisnam pepedit?*

Catch that and sew a button on it!
- *Illud cape et ei fibulam adfige!*

Excuse me, I've got to go take a dump.
- *Ignosce mihi, cacare necesse est.*

Look out, I'm going to barf!
- *Cave, vomiturus sum!*

The Expletives Never Need to Be Deleted in Latin

You've got *stercus* for brains.

You are a complete and total *podex*.

Tete futue and the horse you rode in on.

THE FINE PRINT IS EVEN FINER IN LATIN

Batteries not included.
- *Lagunculae Leydianae non accedunt.*

Void where prohibited by law.
- *Inritum est qua legibus prohibitum est.*

Some restrictions may apply.
- *Forsitan ad hoc aliquot condiciones pertineant.*

Substantial penalty for early withdrawal.
- *Poenas magnas ob depositum praemature postulatum expetimus.*

A CHECKERED PAST IS EASIER TO REVEAL IN LATIN

I've been married before.
- *Matrimonio priore cum altera olim iunctus sum.*

This isn't my real name.
- *Hoc nomen meum verum non est.*

I spent some time in prison.
- *Spatium temporis in carcere egi.*

I don't really know all that much Latin.
- *Re vera, linguam Latinam vix cognovi.*

WIRETAPPERS DON'T KNOW LATIN

Whaddya say we bump him off?
- *Placetne tibi ut eum necemus?*

Let's stick up the joint.
- *Locum despoliemus.*

I got the stuff—you got the money?
- *Materiem habeo—habesne nummos?*

Swell! Hey, you know what I'm gonna do? I'm gonna evade
all the income taxes on it!
- *Bene! At scin quid faciam? Certum est mihi subterfugere omnia
vectigalia ei imposita!*

PILLOW TALK IS MORE ORIGINAL IN LATIN

How was it for you?
- *Quantum placui tibi?*

Did the earth move?
- *Movitne terra, ut ita dicam?*

Was I great, or what?
- *Nonne fui magnificus?*

Want to do it again?
- *Visne iterum agere?*

THINGS YOU SAY IN YOUR SLEEP SOUND LESS RIDICULOUS IN LATIN

I forgot to polish the clocks!
- *Oblitus sum perpolire clepsydras!*

Where's my rubber ducky?
- *Ubi est mea anaticula cumminosa?*

Uh-oh, here comes the lobster man!
- *Eheu, horsum venit vir qui fert locustas!*

Shower shoes! Shower shoes! Shower shoes!
- *Crepidae balneariae! Crepidae balneariae! Crepidae balneariae!*

CERTAIN REQUESTS ARE MORE TACTFULLY COMMUNICATED IN LATIN

Bite my crank.
- *Morde manubrium meum.*

Eat my shorts.
- *Vescere bracis meis.*

Put it where the sun don't shine.
- *Pone ubi sol non lucet.*

TERMS OF NONENDEARMENT

Airhead
Caput vacans

Bimbo
Muliercula

Buttface
Vultus natiformis

Cheese dong
Praeputium

Creep
Cimex

Dolt
Vervex

Doofus
Blennus

Dork
Caudex

Mouthbreather
Hiator

Numbnuts
Testibus torpidis

Sleazeball
Pila foeda

Space cadet
Tiro in exercitu stellarum

Turboslut
Moecha mobilis

Wannabe
Simulator

VI.
GENERAL LATIN
Lingua Latina Generalis

A Latin Chain Letter

This letter has been around the known world many times, and it brings luck wherever it goes. Make ten copies and send them to your friends. Do not break the chain. A person in France broke the chain, and soon after his country was divided into three parts. A general in the Philistines forgot about the letter, and his forces were routed. But Scipio Africanus sent copies of this letter to all the senators in Rome, and the next day he defeated the Carthaginians. Good luck!

• *Haec epistula orbem terrarum cognitarum saepenumero curcumiit et fortunam secundam fert ubicumque eat. Decem exemplaria fac et eos mitte ad amicos. Noli catenam frangere. Homo Gallicus catenam fregit, et patria sua in tres partes brevi post divisa est. Dux ex Philistinis epistulam dedidicit, et copiae suae fusae sunt. Sed Scipio Africanus, exemplaribus epistulae ad senatores Romanos omnes missis, die proximo Carthaginienses vicit. Bona fortuna!*

A Latin Sign for Your Office Desk

COGGITE.
• **THIMK.**

AN ALL-PURPOSE GET-WELL NOTE

I just want you to know that I have sacrificed a good-sized she-goat to Mercury on your behalf in order to hasten your recovery.
PS The entrails were auspicious!
PPS Get well soon!

Volo te scire me capram magnam Mercurio sacrificavisse pro salute tuo celerius restituendo.
PS Exta fausta fuerunt!
PPS Convalesce velociter!

DOCTORS' NOTES ARE MORE CONVINCING IN LATIN

To whom it may concern:
This patient is very sick. He should not go to work under any circumstances. If he feels up to it, he may play a round or two of golf each day, or engage in some similar low-stress activity. He will recover fully, but it's going to take quite some time.

Ei cuius interest:
Hic gravissimo morbo adficitur. Eum oportet haudquaquam laborare. Si se paululum sentiat valescere, ludere lusum Caledonium semel bisve per diem, aut re simili sine sudore operave possit perfungi. E morbo omnino convalescet, sed sibi multo temporis opus erit.

An All-Purpose Letter to the Editor

Dear Blockhead:
Your publication is a scandalous waste of animal hides and papyrus reeds, and your views are unworthy of even the lowliest rabble. If I were emperor (and it may interest you to know that in a previous life I *was*), you'd be sent into exile and spend the rest of your miserable days scribbling bitter diatribes on bits of bark in a smelly hovel in Dalmatia.

Care Baro:
Libellus tuus est iactura probosa pellium papyrique et sententiae tuae indignae etiam plebecula humillima sunt. Si imperator essem (qualis vita priore fui, ut tua fortasse intersit cognoscere), tum tu eiectus in exilium vitam reliquam miserrime degeres scribens Philippicas acerbas in frusta corticis in gurgustio male olenti apud Dalmatas.

AN ALL-PURPOSE RESPONSE TO DUNNING LETTERS FROM SCHOOLS

Dear Sirs:

As you can no doubt tell from my superb Latin, I have dedicated my life to the study of the classics, which, as you probably know, is not a major money-making occupation. Consequently, I am not now, nor will I ever be, able to send you any money. I am certain, however, that any disappointment you might feel at this turn of events is more than compensated for by the great pride you surely have in the scholarly commitment of a former student.

PS Are your diplomas still in Latin?

PPS I think there's a wrong ending in a word in our Latin school motto.

Cari Amici:

Quod haud dubie fit vobis certum ex hac epistula tam eleganter Latine scripta, me dedicavi ad studium litterarum antiquarum, quae, ut fortasse scias bene, negotium non sane quaestuosum est. Ergo, nunc non possum nec umquam potero vobis reddere ullam pecuniam. Pro certo habeo, autem, quemquem dolorem ob illam rem sentiatis omnino compensatum esse ab aestimatione coeptorum eruditorum unius ex vestris discipulis prioribus.

PS Etiamnunc diplomata tua Latine scribuntur?

PPS Credo verbum in nostrae scholae sententia symbolica Latina in falso casu esse.

An All-Purpose Bedtime Story

Once upon a time there were three bears who went for a walk in the woods while their porridge cooled. While they were away, a yellow-haired barbarian girl broke in, ate their food, busted their furniture, and slept in their beds, but when the bears came back, they made a slave of her, and she turned out to be very useful around the house. The end.

Olim erant tres ursi qui in silvas iverant ad ambulandum dum puls sua refrigescat. His absentibus, barbara flava inrupit, escam edit, supellectilem fregit, et in lectis dormivit. Sed cum ursi revenissent, eam in servitutem redegerunt, et ea postea utilissima domi fiebat. Finis.

A Note to Santa

Dear Santa,
I would like a Rolex wristwatch, four Armani suits, and a Ferrari. Thank you.
PS I can name all your reindeer in Latin: Blitzen, Comet, Cupid, Dancer, Dasher, Donder, Prancer, Vixen, and Rudolph the Red-Nosed.

Care Sancte Nicholas,
Aveo horologium manuale Rolicis, quattuor vestitus Armanios, et currum a Ferrario factum. Tibi gratias ago.
PS Scio nomina Latina rangiferorum tuorum omnium: Fulgens, Cometes, Cupido, Saltator, Provolans, Tonitrus, Exsultans, Vulpes, et Rudolphus Naso Rubro.

Handy Acronyms From the Land of SPQR

KISS Keep It Simple, Stupid
- *SSS Sit Simplex, Stulte*

CYA Cover Your Ass
- *PTP Protege Tuam Pugam*

NIMBY Not In My Backyard
- *NPIMV Ne Ponatur In Mea Vicinitate*

MEGO My Eyes Glaze Over
- *OMFL Oculi Mei Fiunt Languidi*

VII.
ESSENTIAL LATIN
Lingua Latina Necessaria

CHANCE ENCOUNTERS ARE LESS AWKWARD IN LATIN

Look what the cat dragged in!
- *Aspice quod felis attraxit!*

Long time no see!
- *Tam diu minime visu!*

Where have you been hiding yourself?
- *Ubi tete occultabas?*

Let's not be strangers!
- *Non simus inter nos advenas!*

See you later, alligator!
- *Vale, lacerte!*

Don't do anything I wouldn't do!
- *Noli aliquid facere quod non faciam!*

Jeepers, what a ying-yang!
- *Edepol, qualem praeputium!*

You Always Have a Leg Up in Latin

I'd like the usual Vatican discount.
- *Volo id ex pretio decrescere quod solet cum Vaticanum nego-tietur.*

Hi. I'm here to pick up the pope's Super Bowl tickets.
- *Ave. Hic adsum ad tesseras pontificis maximi Colosseo Maximo tollendas.*

We'll need an earlier tee time. The archbishop has to get back to the cathedral to judge the Gregorian chant sing-off.
- *Necesse est nobis maturius incipere a "Te." Archiepiscopus debet redire ad ecclesiam cathedralem ut iudicet certamen cantus Gregoriani.*

Affirmations Are More Affirmative in Latin

I'm not just whistling "Dixie"!
- *Non modo sibilo "Terram Dixonis!"*

Does a bear shit in the woods?
- *Cacatne ursus in sylvis?*

Does the pope speak Latin?
- *Loquiturne pontifex maximus Latine?*

Word!
- *Verbum!*

RATIONALIZATIONS ARE MORE RATIONAL IN LATIN

If I hadn't done it, someone else would have.
- *Si id non fecissem, aliquis id fecisset.*

Everyone does it.
- *Sic faciunt omnes.*

What they don't know won't kill them.
- *Quod nesciunt eos non interficiet.*

So what's it to you, anyway?
- *Num curae est tibi?*

A GOOD DEFENSE IS EVEN BETTER IN LATIN

I don't know what you're talking about.
- *Nescio de quo loqueris.*

There's obviously been some sort of silly mistake.
- *Manifesto nescio quis lapsus stultus factus est.*

You must be mad.
- *Vere furis.*

Is this your idea of a joke?
- *Hocine tibi habeas iocum?*

Can you actually prove any of that?
- *Potesne vere ullam partem probare?*

That's my story, and I'm sticking to it.
- *Quae narravi, nullo modo negabo.*

COMEBACKS ARE SNAPPIER IN LATIN

Says who?
• *Quis est qui inquit!*

Is that a fact?
• *Vere dicis!*

T.S.!
• *D.M.!*

So's your old man!
• *Atque vetulus tuus!*

PUT-DOWNS ARE MORE FINAL IN LATIN

Who rattled your cage?
• *Quis caveam tuam quassit!*

Well, pardon me for living.
• *Vae, da mihi veniam vitae.*

Get a life.
• *Fac ut vivas.*

Be real.
• *Veritatem imitare.*

Wake up and smell the coffee.
• *Expergiscere et coffeam olface.*

TALK IS NEVER CHEAP IN LATIN

You're dead meat.
- *Caro putrida es.*

You'll never work in this town again.
- *In hoc oppido nunquam postea operaberis.*

You can run, but you can't hide.
- *Potes currere, sed te occulere non potes.*

Guys like you are a dime a dozen.
- *Capita similia tui aestimantur unius assis.*

I have jerks like you for breakfast.
- *Verveces tui similes pro ientaculo mihi appositi sunt.*

Read it and weep.
- *Lege et lacrima.*

Don't make me laugh.
- *Ne feceris ut rideam.*

I'm shaking, I'm shaking.
- *Pavesco, pavesco.*

SNOW JOBS ARE HOWLING BLIZZARDS IN LATIN

You look marvelous!
- *Quam pulcher/pulchra es!*

How truly fascinating! Do tell me more!
- *Tua verba animum meum tenent! Te precor mihi plus enarrare!*

That's simply divine!
- *Divinissimum est!*

I had a grand time!
- *Me valde oblectavi.*

I shall always cherish the memory of this very, very special occasion.
- *Semper redibo laetus hunc diem praecipuum in memoriam.*

Perhaps a small obelisk could be erected to commemorate it.
- *Forsitan nobis deceat statuere obeliscum parvum ad rem celebrandam.*

You Can Sell Practically Anybody Practically Anything in Latin

Tell you what I'm going to do . . .
- *Mihi permitte tibi dicere quod faciam . . .*

This is a rock-bottom price.
- *Hoc est pretium minimum.*

I'm losing money on this deal.
- *Hoc pacto, pecuniam amitto.*

My boss will kill me when he finds out.
- *Praefectus me e medio tollet quando cognoverit.*

Sign here.
- *Hic signa.*

Next!
- *Propinqua proxime!*

Latin: The Mother of All Tongues

First we're going to cut it off, then we're going to kill it.
- *Primum id abscidemus, tum id occidemus.*

He didn't move it, and now he's going to lose it.
- *Illud non movit, ergo illud perdet.*

I came, I saw, I kicked ass.
- *Veni, vidi, nates calce concidi.*

VIII.
POP-CULTURAL LATIN
Lingua Latina Popularis

ALL COMICS ARE CLASSIC COMICS IN LATIN

It's a bird! It's a plane! It's Superman!
- *Avis est! Aeronavis est! Supervir est!*

Holy subjunctives, Batman!
- *Sanctos subiunctivos, Virvespertilio!*

Oh no, Spidey's having an identity crisis!
- *Eheu, Araneus dubitat qui ipse sit!*

The Hulk broke up with his girlfriend!
- *Moles familiaritatem sibi cum amica dirupit!*

Shazam!
- *Hercule!*

CARTOONS ARE, WELL, CARTOONIER IN LATIN

What's up, Doc?
- *Quid agis, Medice!*

I'll get you, you wascally wabbit!
- *Te capiam, cunicule sceleste!*

I tought I taw a puddy tat!
- *Credidi me felem vidisse!*

Thuffering Thuccotash!
- *Farrago fatigans!*

Beep-beep!
- *Cornu sono!*

Ah-bee, ah-bee, ah-bee, that's all, folks!
- *Abeo, abeo, abeo, actum est, comites!*

The Golden Age of TV Would Have Been Even More Golden in Latin

Just the facts, ma'am.
- *Dic mihi solum facta, domina.*

Sorry about that, chief.
- *Illius me paenitet, dux.*

You bet your bippy!
- *Tuis pugis pignore!*

The devil made me do it!
- *Diabolus fecit, ut id facerem!*

Kiss my grits!
- *Osculare pultem meam!*

Beam me up, Scotty!
- *Me transmitte sursum, Caledoni!*

If you fail, the secretary will disavow all knowledge of your activities.
- *Si fallatis officium, quaestor infitias eat se quicquam scire de factis vestris.*

You'd Have Been Allowed to Listen to the Radio All Night If Only It Had Been in Latin

What's behind that creaking door?
- *Quid pone illud ostium crepans situm est?*

The Shadow knows.
- *Umbra scit.*

Who was that masked man?
- *Quis fuit ille personatus?*

Hi-ho, Silver, away!
- *Eeia, Argentei, eamus!*

Good night, Mrs. Calabash, wherever you are.
- *Vale, era Curcurbita, ubicumque sis.*

THE ALL-TIME TOP X

I Heard It Through the Grapevine
- *Hoc Fama Mihi, Cursum Sinuosum Secuta, Nuntiat*

Itsy Bitsy Teeny Weenie Yellow Polka Dot Bikini
- *Ceston atque Cingulum Parvissimos Minutissimos Natatorios Flavos Ocellatos*

The 59th Street Bridge Song (Feelin' Groovy)
- *Cantus Pontis Viae Undesexagesimae (Laetans)*

Stop in the Name of Love
- *Siste in Nomine Amoris*

Shake, Rattle, and Roll
- *Treme, Strepe, et Volutare*

These Boots Are Made for Walking
- *Caligae ad Ambulandum Factae Sunt*

Be True to Your School
- *Fidelis Scholae Tuae Esto*

You Can't Always Get What You Want
- *Non Potes Semper Capere Quod Aves*

Diamonds on the Soles of Her Shoes
- *Sunt Adamantes in Solis Calceorum Suorum*

Everybody's Got Something to Hide Except for Me and My Monkey
- *Habent Abdenda Omnes Praeter Me ac Simiam Meam*

WRITE YOUR OWN LATIN B-MOVIE SCRIPT

Huge flying discuses have landed in the Campus Martius!
- *Orbes immanes volantes in Campum Martium advenerunt!*

It's horrible! These creatures have the head of a lizard and the body of a Helvetian!
- *Horribile dictu! His animalibus biformibus sunt caput lacerti iunctum ad corpus Helvetii!*

Our weapons are useless against them!
- *Tela nostra nihil nobis prosunt in illos.*

Send for the Greek thinker! Perhaps he can save us with his arcane arts!
- *Arcesse Palameden! Forsitan possit nos servare artibus suis abditis!*

It's MMMMMMM to I, but it's our only chance—a flame-hurling catapult!
- *Cum sit periculum tremendum, res tamen in aleam nobis danda est—ecce catapulta quae liquorem ardentem iacit!*

It's so crazy it just might work!
- *Tam insulsum est ut fortasse expediat.*

Incredible! The Greek fire is melting them like wax!
- *Incredibile est! Ignis Graecus illos dissolvit quasi e cera facti sint!*

Is it The End, or The Beginning of The End, or The End of The Beginning, or The Beginning . . . ?
- *Estne Finis, aut Initium Finis, aut Finis Initii, aut Initium . . . !*

THE SEVEN DWARFS GAIN MORE STATURE IN LATIN

Dopey
Fatuus

Doc
Medicullus

Grumpy
Severus

Happy
Beatus

Sleepy
Somniculosus

Bashful
Verecundus

Sneezy
Sternuens

NOSTALGIA IS MORE NOSTALGIC IN LATIN

Let's have a Tupperware party!
* *Habeamus convivium ad mercem emendam Tupperi!*

Let's turn on the lava lamp!
* *Accendamus lucernam plenam massae ardentis!*

Let's all wear mood rings!
* *Anulos qui animum ostendunt omnes gestemus!*

Let's have a sock hop!
* *In tibialibus saltemus!*

IMMORTAL HEADLINES FROM *THE CLASSICAL ENQUIRER*

PUER PATREM CAEDIT, MATREM SUAM IN MATRIMONIUM DUCIT
- YOUTH KILLS HIS DAD, MARRIES OWN MOM

CUM BELUA BARBARA IN LABYRINTHO NEFANDO PUGNAT: SEMIVIR, SEMIBOS CARNEM HUMANAM EDIT
- HE BATTLES WEIRD BEAST IN HELLISH MAZE: HALF-MAN, HALF-BULL DINED ON HUMAN FLESH

REX DEMENS INFANTES FRATRIS SUI INTERFICIT COQUITQUE, TUM CENAM FOEDAM PARENTI HORRIFICATO APPONIT
- MAD KING SLAYS AND COOKS HIS BROTHER'S TOTS, THEN SERVES LOATHSOME DISH TO TYKES' HORRIFIED POP

IX.
COMMERCIAL LATIN
Lingua Latina Mercatoria

BE YOUR OWN AD EXEC WITH LINGO FROM THE VIA MADISONIS

Let's run it up the flagpole and see if anybody salutes it!
- *Id in summum longurium quasi vexillum tollamus ut videamus utrum quis id salutet, necne!*

Let's put it in the Colosseum and see if the lions will eat it!
- *Id in Colosseo ponamus ut videamus utrum leones id edant, necne!*

Let's divide it into three parts and see if anybody conquers it!
- *Id in tres partes dividamus ut videamus utrum quis id vincat, necne!*

Let's make it emperor and see if anybody assassinates it in the Forum!
- *Id imperatorem faciamus ut videamus utrum quis in Foro id interficiat, necne!*

Immortal Tag Lines Are Even More Classic in Latin

It takes a tough man to make a tender chicken.
• *Solus fortis et durus pullum tenerum parare potest.*

Tastes great! Less filling!
• *Iucunde sapit! Minime implet!*

I can't believe I ate the whole thing.
• *Non possum credere me totum edisse.*

It's ugly, but it gets you there.
• *Deformis est, sed te illuc fert.*

Where's the beef?
• *Ubi est bubula?*

Moronic Tag Lines Are Slightly More Bearable in Latin

Please don't squeeze the Charmin!
• *Sis, noli Volvivoluptatem comprimere!*

It's the quicker picker-upper.
• *Tollit velocius.*

I liked the shaver so much, I bought the company.
• *Tantum novaculam amabam, societatem emi.*

My wife—I think I'll keep her.
• *Uxor mea—Credo me eam semper retenturum.*

Just do it.
• *Modo fac.*

THE OLDEST JINGLES SOUND BRAND-NEW IN LATIN

Double your pleasure, double your fun, with double good, double fresh Doublemint gum!
- *Duplica gaudia tua et delectamenta, bis bona, bis nova, gummi Diplomentha!*

Hold the pickles, hold the lettuce! Special orders don't upset us, at McDonald's!
- *Parce cucumeris frustis! Parce lactucae! Mandata peculiaria nobis non sunt oneri, apud Filium Donaldi!*

Call Roto-Rooter—that's the name—and away go troubles down the drain!
- *Vocate Purgatorem Versabundum—nomen est nobis—et in cloacas abluemus calamitates quae sunt vobis!*

Gaudeat Emptor! (Let the Buyer Rejoice!)

Shake 'n Bake
Quate et Coque

Roast'n Boast
Torre ac Gloriare

Pop Tarts
Scriblitae Exsilientes

Devil Dogs
Crusti Diaboli

Rice-a-Roni
Oryza Mixta

Tuna Helper
Adiutor Thunni

Fish sticks
Piscilli

Sloppy Joes
Iosephi Inconditi

Fig Newtons
Crustuli Ficulnei

Chips Ahoy
Ave Assulae

Handy Wipes
Mantelia Habilia

Ty-D-Bol
Matula Nitida

Sweet 'n Low
Dulce Leveque

Tender Vittles
Esca Tenera

Kibbles 'n' Bits
Frusti et Gustuli

Pampers
Indulgentes

Miracle Whip
Confusio Mirifica

Roach Motels
Cauponae Blattariae

Yard Guard
Custodia Propatuli

Jujubes
Zizypha

X.
CELEBRATIONAL LATIN
Lingua Latina Festiva

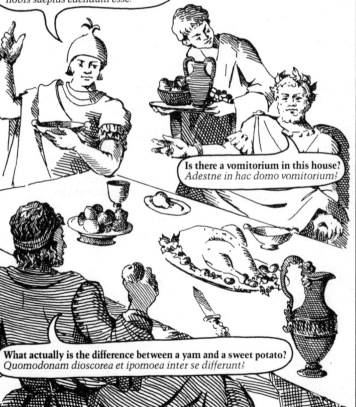

THINGS TO SAY ON YOUR BIRTHDAY

Happy Birthday to me!
- *Diem natalem felicem mihi!*

For me? You shouldn't have!
- *Mihi? Opus non fuit!*

I never would have guessed!
- *Nunquam coniectaverim!*

It's just what I wanted!
- *Est admodum quod volui!*

Where on earth did you find it?
- *Ubi gentium illud invenisti?*

Do you happen to know offhand what their policy is on returns?
- *Scisne forte quid soleant agere cum res reductis?*

THINGS TO SAY AT A BAR MITZVAH

This is delicious. What is it?
- *Iucunde sapit. Quid est?*

May I have some more smoked salmon?
- *Da mihi, sis, plus salmonis fumosi.*

THINGS TO SAY ON GROUNDHOG DAY

How do you know you have the right groundhog?
- *Ut scis te observare marmotam monacem ipsam?*

What happens if he wanders out on a highway and gets run over by a truck? Do we get an ice age?
- *Quid fiat si in viam erret et a vehiculo magno conculcetur? Saeclum glaciale?*

LATIN VALENTINES FOR ST. VALENTINE'S DAY

Roses are red, violets are blue,
Gaul is divided into three parts,
And so will my heart be if I ever lose you!

*Rubore di tinxerunt rosas
Caeruleo di tinxerunt violas
Cor meum in partes tres dividatur si tu me umquam relinquas!*

Roses are red, violets are blue,
I don't care if the Carthaginians keep Carthage,
So long as I always have you!

*Rubore di tinxerunt rosas,
Caeruleo di tinxerunt violas
Ita Carthaginienses Carthaginem habere possint ut semper habeam meas delicias!*

Things to Say on St. Patrick's Day

Erin, go bragh!
- *Hibernia in aeternum!*

If I drink this funny-looking beer, will my pee turn green, too?
- *Si bibam hanc cerevesiam, quae speciem insolitam praebet, urinane mea eveniet quoque viridans!*

May all your nouns and adjectives agree in gender and number. . . .
- *Nomina omnia et nomina adiectiva tua in genere et numero congruant. . . .*

May you always use the subjunctive properly. . . .
- *Modo subiunctivo recte utaris. . . .*

And may you never accidentally try out your Latin on a Jesuit.
- *Et casu Latine loqui cum sodale Societatis Jesu ne umquam conaris.*

Things to Say at Easter

If he's the Easter *Bunny*, where does he get the eggs?
- *Si Cuniculus Paschalis sit, unde ova capiat!*

Maybe they're really brought by the Easter Lizard or the Easter Snake.
- *Forsitan re ipsa Lacerta Paschalis vel Anguis Paschalis illa ferat.*

HANDY MESSAGES FOR EVERYONE'S LEAST FAVORITE HOLIDAYS

Dear Mom:
I know I never write, I know I never call,
I'm really most contrite, but I've been very busy in Gaul.
Happy Mother's Day.

Cara mater mea:
Scio me tibi non unquam scribere, scio me tibi non filo dicere,
Huius me valde paenitebat, sed mihi in Gallia opus erat.
Felici die maternali fruere.

Dear Dad:
I'm not too proud to pen it: You never got your due.
That's why I've asked the Senate to name a salad for you.
Happy Father's Day.

Care pater mi:
Vere, id mihi scribendum est: Multum tibi debendum est.
Igitur cogito Senatum rogare acetaria ex te rite appellare.
Felici die paternali fruere.

THINGS TO SAY AT GRADUATION

Hey, this diploma is in English!
• *Vae! Hoc diploma Anglice scriptum est!*

Gyp! Gyp! I want my money back!
• *Fraudem! Fraudem! Mea pecunia vobis redenda est!*

THINGS TO SAY ON THE FOURTH OF JULY

Wow! Did you see that one?
- *Hercle! Illud vidistine?*

Look! This one's going to be even bigger!
- *Aspice! Hoc etiam grandius erit!*

Oooooooooo!
- *Uuuuuuuuuu!*

THINGS TO SAY ON HALLOWEEN

Trick or Treat!
- *Dolus vel dulce!*

Sorry, kids, all I have is olives and figs.
- *Mihi paenitet, pueri, sed nihil aliud habeo nisi olivas et ficos.*

What do you mean, "nice costume"? This is my best toga!
- *Quid vis dicere, "vestitus theatralis suavis"? Haec est mea toga optima!*

That mask isn't very scary. Have you ever seen a Helvetian?
- *Larva illa non est formidolosior. Umquam vidisti Helvetium?*

Do you know what a catapult is?
- *Novistisne quid sit catapulta?*

If you're thinking of putting toilet paper on my house, ask yourself if you can outrun a ninety-mile-an-hour rock.
- *Si in animis habeatis scidam latrinariam in domo mea ponere, vosmet rogate si possitis velocius currere quam saxum quod vadit cum celeritate nonaginta milia passuum per horam.*

THINGS TO SAY AT THANKSGIVING

I'd like to help, but I only know how to cut up birds for
    purposes of augury.
- *Cum velim te iuvare, solum tamen scio aves secare ad
augurandum.*

What actually is the difference between a yam and a sweet
    potato?
- *Quomodonam dioscorea et ipomoea inter se differunt?*

You know, we really ought to have turkey more often.
- *Opinor vere meleagridem gallopavonem nobis saepius edendum
esse.*

I'll have some more mashed potatoes and gravy.
- *Da mihi, amabo, plus solanorum tuberosorum tunsorum et iuris.*

Oh boy, pumpkin pie!
- *Euax, crustum cucurbitae peponis!*

Um, do you by any chance happen to have a vomitorium in
    this house?
- *En, habeasne forte in hac domo vomitorium?*

THINGS TO SAY ON HANUKKAH

Happy Hanukkah!
- *Hanukka felicem vobis!*

So enough already with the Latin-Schmatin, let's eat.
- *Iam est satis superque linguae Latinae-Fatuinae. Edamus.*

THINGS TO SAY AT CHRISTMAS

Bah! Humbug!
- *Phy! Fabulae!*

Christmas has gotten too commercial.
- *Dies natalis Christi nimis mercatoria facta est.*

I'll have some more of that eggnog.
- *Sumam plus oögalactos.*

So, who do you like for the Super Bowl?
- *Bene, cui in Colosseo Maximo faves?*

NEW YEAR'S RESOLUTIONS ARE LESS BINDING IN LATIN

This year I am definitely going to . . .
- *Hoc anno ego pro certo . . .*

> go on a diet.
> *diaetam sequi incipiam.*
>
> get more exercise.
> *musculos saepius exercebo.*
>
> attend more cultural events.
> *adsidue bonis artibus studere.*
>
> make larger charitable contributions.
> *liberalius largiar.*
>
> be nicer to people.
> *benignius aliis me geram.*
>
> stop misusing the subjunctive.
> *abuti modo subiunctivo desinam.*

A BRIEF GUIDE TO
LATIN PRONUNCIATION

Locutio Linguae Latinae
Paucis Verbis Explanatur

If it's been a few years since you last conversed in Latin regularly, your pronunciation may have gotten a bit rusty, so we've included here a short summary of the basics of the spoken language just to help you brush up a little.

A word of caution: This is a simplified system of pronunciation for colloquial Latin based in part on modern Italian, the direct vernacular descendant of the everyday speech of ancient Rome. If you're planning to give a formal oration or a reading from one of the great works of classical literature, you're obviously going to want to consult the standard scholarly reference books for the proper literary pronunciation.

I VOWELS AND A FEW DIPHTHONGS

Sure, I speak a little Latin.
• *Sane, paululum linguae Latinae dico.*
  SAH-nay, pow-LOO-luhm LEEN-gwye Lah-TEE-nye DEE-koh.

A   is pronounced "ah" as in "father."
E   is pronounced "ay" as in "they," but the very common words et (and), est (is), and sed (but) should be pronounced like "bet," "best," and "said," and the very common word ending em should be pronounced like "stem."

I   is pronounced "ee" as in "Vaseline," but the very common words <u>i</u>d (it) and <u>i</u>n (in, on) should be pronounced like "<u>di</u>d" and "<u>di</u>n."

O   is pronounced "oh" as in "g<u>o</u>."

U   is pronounced "oo" as in "cr<u>u</u>de," but the very common word endings <u>us</u> and <u>um</u> should be pronounced like "p<u>u</u>ss" and "r<u>oo</u>m" (with the "oo" sound of "c<u>oo</u>kb<u>oo</u>k"), and the very common word <u>ut</u> (how, so that) should be pronounced like "p<u>u</u>t."

AE is a diphthong (a pair of vowels joined together to form a single sound) pronounced "eye."

AU is a diphthong pronounced "ow," as in "l<u>uau</u>."

OE is a diphthong pronounced "oy."

II CONSONANTS

I picked it up here and there. Really, Latin isn't all that hard.

• *Id legi modo hic modo illic. Vero, Latine loqui non est difficilius.*

IDD LAY-gee MOH-doh HEEK MOH-doh EEL-leek. WAY-roh, Lah-TEE-nay LOH-kwee NOHN EHSST dee-fee-KEE-lee-uss.

B, D, F, H, K, L, M, N, P, and Z all sound the same as they do in English.

C   always has a "K" sound as in "<u>c</u>ar."

Ch   always has a "K" sound as in "<u>ch</u>orus."

G   always has a hard "G" sound as in "<u>g</u>et."

Gu   is pronounced "Gw" when it comes after an "n," as it is in "lan<u>gu</u>age."

I   is a consonant pronounced like "Y" when it is the first letter in a word and it is followed by a vowel. The common Latin word <u>iam</u> (now) is pronounced "YAHM."

Qu   is pronounced "Kw," just as in English.

R   can be rolled in a sort of Scottish burr.

S   always has a hissing sound as in "moose" or "soda," and some very common word endings sound like this: <u>as</u> = "demitasse"; <u>es</u> = "ace"; <u>is</u> = "geese"; <u>os</u> = "verb<u>ose</u>"; and <u>us</u> = "<u>wuss</u>."

T   always has a hard "T" sound as in "<u>t</u>ar." In Latin, the word "ratio" is pronounced "RAH-tee-oh."

V   is always pronounced as if it were a "W." What Caesar (KYE-sahr) said after he defeated somebody or other (*veni, vidi, vici*) sounded as if he had just conquered Hawaii: WAY-nee, WEE-dee, WEE-kee.*

X   is always pronounced "Ks."

J, W, and Y don't exist in Latin.

III   Syllables

It looks like a tricky language, but you'll get the hang of it pretty quickly.

- *Lingua speciem involutam praebet, sed sat cito eam comprehendes.*

LEEN-gwah   SPAY-kee-ehm   inn-woh-LOO-tahm   PRYE-bayt, SEDD SAHT KEE-toh AY-ahm kohm-pray-HAYN-dace.

Latin words are divided into syllables in the same way that English words are, but in Latin every vowel or diphthong is a syllable, and every syllable is pronounced separately. If there are two vowels together, and they are not AE, AU, or OE, both vowels are pronounced individually. So, for example, <u>praebat</u> = "PRYE-baht" (ae is a diphthong); <u>speciem</u> = "SPAY-kee-ehm"; and <u>eam</u> = "AY-ahm."

---

* If you took Latin in a parochial school, you were probably taught to pronounce the letter "V" like the English "V," the dipthong "ae" like "sundae", and Caesar like "CHAY-sahr." If you do this, you are going to take <u>some</u> flak from Latin purists, classics snobs, and other assorted lingo bores, but on the other hand, you're going to get a much better table in the Vatican restaurant.

IV STRESS

And remember, there aren't any Romans around to correct
    your pronunciation.
- *Atque memento, nulli adsunt Romanorum qui locutionem tuam*
    corrigant.

AHT-kway may-MAYN-toh, NOO-lee AHD-soont Roh-mah-
    NOH-ruhm KWEE loh-koo-tee-OH-nehm TOO-ahm KOH-ree-
    gahnt.

If a word has two syllables, put the stress on the first one. If it has
more than two, put the stress on the second-to-last syllable unless
both the second-to-last syllable and the last syllable are vowels.
When that happens, shift the stress back one syllable earlier.

So, for example, <u>locutionem</u> = "loh-koo-tee-OH-nehm," but <u>lo-
cutio</u> = "loh-KOO-tee-oh."

If the second-to-last syllable has an "i" in it and doesn't end in
a consonant, the stress is usually moved back one syllable. So, for
example, <u>corrigant</u> = "KOHR-ree-gahnt" and <u>difficilius</u> = "dee-
fee-KEE-lee-uss." For the same reason, the very common word <u>ali-
qui</u> (any) is pronounced "AH-lee-kwee."